Praise for *The Gospel According to RFK*

"Some of the most exhilarating days in American life occurred between March 16, 1968, when Robert Kennedy announced his presidential campaign and June 4, 1968, when he was assassinated. Both the hopes and fears of those 81 days are captured in this exhilarating book. Kennedy's anger over hunger, his passion against the war in Vietnam and his faith in black Americans are recorded in 23 unforgettable chapters. Those who read this inspiring volume will acquire a deeper admiration and gratitude for Bobby Kennedy than they ever had before."

—ROBERT F. DRINAN, S.J., PROFESSOR,
GEORGETOWN UNIVERSITY LAW CENTER

"RFK, in his brief 1968 campaign, inspired us to be a better nation and to challenge ourselves. He gave us hope in our hearts, not the facade of religious piety that has no heart. Reading his speeches from that period, it is painful to realize what we lost—and how America has been stumbling in the fog all these many years. For all their talk of morality, the Busheviks have built an elitist, incompetent monarchy that is dependent on appealing to the most base instincts of Americans, whatever their lofty rhetoric. RFK challenged us to reach for the stars, not stare at the abyss."

—*BUZZFLASH*

"A badly needed corrective offering compassion, understanding, and optimism and providing an alternative way of dealing with the pessimism and despair fed to us daily by the present administration."

—VINE DELORIA, JR., AUTHOR OF *CUSTER DIED FOR YOUR SINS*

"Gleaned from campaign speeches of March 16, 1968 through June 4, 1968, the compelling words of Robert F. Kennedy ring out as a reminder from the past, a prod on our conscience, and a call to action. Recommended reading for anyone who has forgotten or would like to newly acquire the faith in American democracy that was Robert F. Kennedy."

—*THE COMPASS*

"In the 1960s, there were two ministers who were preaching to us. One was Martin Luther King and the other was the Reverend Robert F. Kennedy, who was telling us what the right thing to do was. And I know as an Irish Catholic in the 1960s that his was the church I was praying in, but you needed to hear the words from him so that you knew what the right thing to do was. What Norman MacAfee has done is to write a book that has captured all this wisdom."

—MASSACHUSETTS REPRESENTATIVE EDWARD MARKEY,
INTRODUCING NORMAN MACAFEE AT THE
RECEPTION CELEBRATING RFK'S 80TH BIRTHDAY,
AT THE U.S. CAPITOL, NOVEMBER 18, 2005

The Gospel According to RFK: Why it Matters Now should be required reading for all of today's progressives (and probably for all high school students). . . . After reading this book, I could understand how Bobby Kennedy represented, more than anything else, hope. His words are truly moving. His loss a terrible tragedy."

—DAILY KOS

"This collection of excerpts from the speeches Robert F. Kennedy gave when he ran for president in 1968 resound with idealism and a vision for a compassionate world."

—PUBLISHER'S WEEKLY

"The best book for converting your Republican friends to our side: *The Gospel According to RFK* by Norman MacAfee."

—THE DEMOCRATIC DAILY

THE GOSPEL ACCORDING TO RFK

Why It Matters Now

Edited and with Commentary by
NORMAN MACAFEE

New, Revised, and Expanded Edition
Commemorating the 40th Anniversary
of Robert Kennedy's 1968
Presidential Campaign

BASIC
BOOKS

A Member of the Perseus Books Group
New York

Books published by Basic Books are available at special discounts for bulk
purchases in the United States by corporations, institutions, and other
organizations. For more information, please contact the Special Markets
Department at the Perseus Books Group, 2300 Chestnut Street, Suite 200,
Philadelphia, PA 19103, call (800) 255-1514, or e-mail
special.markets@perseusbooks.com.

A Cataloging-in-Publication data record for this book available from the
Library of Congress.
Hardcover ISBN: 0-8133-9157-1
Paperback ISBN: 978-0-465-00358-7
10   9   8   7   6   5   4   3   2   1

Contents

Introduction   1

1   *"These are not ordinary times and this is not an ordinary election"*   13
    WASHINGTON, D.C., MARCH 16, 1968

2   *Ending the War*   21
    KANSAS STATE UNIVERSITY, MANHATTAN, KANSAS, MARCH 18, 1968

3   *The Other America*   39
    UNIVERSITY OF KANSAS, LAWRENCE, KANSAS, MARCH 18, 1968

4   *Dissent in Time of War*   47
    VANDERBILT UNIVERSITY, NASHVILLE, TENNESSEE, MARCH 21, 1968

5   *National Reconciliation*   53
    UNIVERSITY OF ALABAMA, TUSCALOOSA, ALABAMA, MARCH 21, 1968

6   *California Rallies*   59
    CALIFORNIA, MARCH 23, 1968; GREEK THEATRE, LOS ANGELES, MARCH 24, 1968

7 *The Grand Alliance*   *69*
SALINAS/MONTEREY, CALIFORNIA, MARCH 24, 1968

8 *". . . through the eyes of the poor"*   *73*
OLVERA STREET, LOS ANGELES, CALIFORNIA, MARCH 24, 1968

9 *The Spirit of the Young*   *79*
WEBER STATE COLLEGE, OGDEN, UTAH, MARCH 27, 1968

10 *Johnson Withdraws*   *85*
NEW YORK CITY, APRIL 1,1968

11 *Community Development*   *89*
BEDFORD-STUYVESANT, NEW YORK, APRIL 1, 1968

12 *On the Death of Martin Luther King, Jr.*   *95*
INDIANAPOLIS, INDIANA, APRIL 4, 1968

13 *On the Mindless Menace of Violence*   *101*
CLEVELAND, OHIO, APRIL 5, 1968

14 *In Black America*   *107*
FORT WAYNE, INDIANA, APRIL 10, 1968; MICHIGAN STATE
UNIVERSITY, EAST LANSING, MICHIGAN, APRIL 11, 1968

15 *The Art of Peace*   *117*
PORTLAND, OREGON, APRIL 17, 1968

16 *Celebration in Brooklyn*   *125*
BEDFORD-STUYVESANT, NEW YORK, APRIL 18, 1968

17 *Ending Hunger and Malnutrition*   *129*
WASHINGTON, D.C., APRIL 23, 1968

18 *No More Vietnams*   *133*
INDIANA UNIVERSITY, BLOOMINGTON, INDIANA, APRIL 24, 1968

CONTENTS

19 *Health Care*   *139*
INDIANA UNIVERSITY MEDICAL SCHOOL, INDIANAPOLIS, INDIANA,
APRIL 26, 1968

20 *The American Farmland*   *145*
OTOE COUNTY COURTHOUSE, NEBRASKA CITY, NEBRASKA,
MAY 10, 1968; BROOKINGS, SOUTH DAKOTA, MAY 11, 1968

21 *The Question of Welfare*   *151*
PRESS RELEASE, MAY 19, 1968

22 *The New Politics*   *157*
SAN FRANCISCO, CALIFORNIA, MAY 21, 1968

23 *Cleaning Our Air and Our Waters*   *163*
PRESS RELEASE, MAY 26, 1968

24 *Victory*   *169*
LOS ANGELES, CALIFORNIA, JUNE 4, 1968

ACKNOWLEDGMENTS   181
NOTES   183
BIBLIOGRAPHY   189
INDEX   193

"Together we can make ourselves a nation that spends more on books than on bombs, more on hospitals than the terrible tools of war, more on decent houses than military aircraft."
RFK, MARCH 24, 1968

"It's class, not color. What everyone wants is a job and some hope."
RFK, IN CONVERSATION AT DINNER A FEW DAYS
BEFORE THE INDIANA PRIMARY, MAY 7, 1968

"The civil rights leader and Congressman John Lewis once said: 'When Robert F. Kennedy was assassinated, something died in America. Something died in all of us.' If that something is to be reborn, we must first dredge up something too long forgotten in our politics: heart. We must appeal to the compassion and goodness of America and stir the souls of the people so that once again they will believe in the possibility that our country can change—rapidly and profoundly."
ARIANNA HUFFINGTON, FANATICS AND FOOLS:
THE GAME PLAN FOR WINNING BACK AMERICA

Introduction

I T IS FORTY YEARS now since the assassination of Senator Robert
Francis Kennedy. In many ways he was the greatest president
we never had. During the 81 days of his presidential campaign,
from March 16 to June 4, 1968, RFK envisioned a way out of perpetual war and perpetual poverty. His murder sent a message of
hopelessness, that nothing was possible anymore. And the country began its forty-year lurch to the right, to vast income disparity
and preemptive wars.

1968 was one of the two or three most extraordinary years of
the twentieth century. Early in the year, people power in Czechoslovakia brought in a new progressive president, Alexander
Dubcek. In Paris in May, students and workers began demonstrations that would change the culture of Europe for decades. In
Vietnam, Ho Chi Minh's nationalist government was continuing
to draw inspiration from the American, French, Russian, and Chi-
nese revolutions. In the United States, a youth revolution was un-
derway of rock and roll, hallucinogenic drugs, long hair, street
theater, radical thought, sexual freedom, liberation politics, radical

writing, and antiwar activism. In New York, in April, 90,000 people filled Central Park to protest the Vietnam war, and a student strike shut down Columbia University, which only a police riot could reopen.

In America, it all had the feel of a revolution. It wasn't a classic national revolution in the sense of one group overthrowing another. But there were pervasive revolutions within society, especially the civil rights revolution. There were revolutions in ways of thinking. 1968 was the year that the term "black" replaced "Negro," and you can see the chronological transformation of the term in the speeches in this volume. We would have to wait a few more years before "man" and "he" were replaced with more gender-friendly usages for humanity in general, male and female.

1968 was an election year, the year President Lyndon Johnson should have been reelected on a platform of his Great Society and War on Poverty programs. But he was fighting a massive war with all the weapons of a superpower against the small country of Vietnam. Nineteen thousand American soldiers and a million Vietnamese were already dead in that war. Amid all this—revolution in the winds, revulsion against the war—on March 16, 1968, Robert Kennedy announced his candidacy for the presidency.

As he campaigned across the country, Kennedy outlined a redemptive vision for America and the world that rings true today. *The Gospel According to RFK* tells the story of Kennedy's campaign and its ideas through excerpts from his speeches. We see him reasoning that the war in Vietnam is destroying the country it was supposed to save, and that the war has to end without American victory. We see him telling college students that their draft defer-ments are unfair, forcing other young men, usually poor and working class, who could not afford college, to fight and perhaps to die in Vietnam. We see him outlining plans to help communi-ties get out of poverty and stay out. We see him championing Native Americans and migrant workers. The subjects of these speeches read like a litany of what we must do now: end the war; decrease the gap between rich and poor; honor the importance of dissent especially in time of war; repair the damage done to our relations with our allies because of the war; create a new politics of greater participation; build successful communities in poor areas; protect our natural resources; increase the number of small farms; and eliminate classism and racism.

Kennedy realized that the greatest domestic problem was in-come inequality, not skin color: "It's class, not color. What every-one wants is a job and some hope."[1] Because of this insight, this understanding, he was "wildly cheered by angry blacks, then cheered with equal enthusiasm by blue-collar whites who pro-fessed to hate blacks,"[2] making for a potentially transformative alliance that has gone unrepresented since his death. Since 1968, although blacks and Hispanics have more rights, the gap between rich and poor is far vaster than it was then. In the 1960s, the ratio between the average salaries of the heads of companies and the workers in them was 20 to 1; now it is 400 to 1.[3]

RFK was acquainted with sorrow and pain. After the assassina-tion of his brother, President John Fitzgerald Kennedy, in 1963, RFK sought solace in the Greek classics and the writings of the

New England Transcendentalist Ralph Waldo Emerson and the French existentialist Albert Camus. As one of RFK's biographers, Evan Thomas, writes: "He became an existentialist without at the same time abandoning his faith in God. . . . He had been a romantic Catholic who believed it was possible to create the Kingdom of Heaven on earth. He lost the certainty of his faith but never the hope. . . . [Camus] helped Kennedy deal with pain and inevitability. Kennedy was immensely relieved to read Camus's message that the absurdity and seeming meaninglessness of life is not an end but rather a beginning, that because life is so wretchedly unpredictable and uncontrollable, it is up to each man to start his life anew each day."[4] Because he felt this sorrow, he knew what was most important for most of humanity: make a world where there is less and less unnecessary pain and suffering.

As the writer David Talbot has pointed out, President Kennedy "often said he wanted his epitaph to be 'He kept the peace.'"[5] And RFK treasured a note from his brother's last cabinet meeting, in which JFK had scribbled the word "poverty" and circled it several times.[6] After President Kennedy's death, peace and social justice became the younger Kennedy's guiding stars. Without peace there can be none of the good things of life. We must start there, and then build a great society. JFK's vice president and successor, Lyndon Johnson, thought you could have both an unjust war and social justice.

On April 4, Kennedy was about to address a political rally in a black neighborhood in Indianapolis when he learned that Martin Luther King, Jr., had been assassinated. In one of the most beautiful of all extemporaneous American speeches, RFK breaks the terrible news to the crowd. He quotes the ancient Greek playwright: "My favorite poet was Aeschylus. He wrote: 'In our sleep, pain which cannot forget falls drop by drop upon the heart until, in our own despair, against our will, comes wisdom through the awful grace of God.'" For Kennedy, the wisdom he gained from the suffering he saw around him, as well as the pain he experienced at the assassination of his brother, comes down to this, I think: We must do everything we can to help those who have the least. As Martin Luther King's widow, Coretta, said of RFK and JFK, "Although they were political figures, they were human beings first, and their humanness reached out to the needs of people."[7]

Robert Kennedy's moral fervor, the idea of redeeming humanity through equality and justice, was a mixture of religion and politics enacted in an ecumenical world where Pope John XXIII provided the moral compass and Che Guevara the revolutionary fervor. In some ways, RFK and Martin Luther King combined the two sides. In his magisterial biography, *Robert Kennedy and His Times,* Arthur Schlesinger, Jr., quotes Alice Roosevelt Longworth, Theodore Roosevelt's daughter: "Bobby could have been a revolutionary priest."[8] Another of RFK's biographers, Jack Newfield, describes his amazing empathy: "Kennedy had the almost literary ability to put himself inside other people, to see the world with the eyes of its casualties. A friend once said, 'I think Bobby knows precisely what it feels like to be a very old woman.' In November of 1965 Kennedy went down into one of the miserable coal mines of Lota, Chile, where most of the miners belong to a communist union. When he came up, he told a reporter, 'If I worked in this mine, I'd be a Communist, too.'"[9] The head of the farmworkers union, his friend César Chávez, said, "He could see things through the eyes of the poor." In the days after RFK's death, Schlesinger, who was a close adviser to both John and Robert Kennedy, tried to sum up the difference between them: "JFK, one sensed, was always a skeptic and an ironist; he had understood the complexity of things since birth. RFK began as a true believer; he acquired his sense of the complexity of things from hard experience. He remained a true believer to the end but at a far deeper level; he had long since chucked away the eternal criteria and received simplifications and got down as far as one can in politics to the human meaning of things."[10]

Robert Kennedy's death was a disaster for progressive politics in America and around the world. He had a good chance of getting the Democratic nomination and winning the election. He campaigned on ending the war soon after his inauguration through negotiation, not escalation, and we could expect the war to have ended by late 1969. Then, the opportunities forgone because of the war could have been seized: narrowing the gap between rich and poor, making headway in health care, education, and all the other things that make life good. Instead, Johnson's vice president, former Minnesota senator Hubert Humphrey, won the nomination, but enough Democratic votes went to the racist third-party candidacy of George Wallace, cutting into the Southern Democratic vote, to narrowly elect Richard Nixon. The Vietnam War continued for another seven years—through Watergate and the resignation of Nixon under threat of impeachment, and into the presidency of Gerald Ford. In the end, 3.2 million Vietnamese and 58,000 Americans were killed in the war, two-thirds of them dead after 1968. And the United States, which had started the war, lost it.

President Nixon went on to sponsor coups in Chile, destroying democracy there for twenty years, and in Cambodia. Onto that neutral country, widening the war in Vietnam, he unleashed the most intensive bombing in history up to that time. The daily devastation from the sky drove Cambodians—a traditionally peace-loving, cultured people—insane, if a people can be said to go insane, and led to the genocide of millions under Pol Pot. None of this would have happened under RFK. Of course, beyond a few years after 1969, it becomes hard to hypothesize what the world would look like. It is up to readers to imagine that world, to fill in the blanks, if they wish.

Besides politics, *The Gospel According to RFK* exists on other levels that expand the nation's moral vocabulary. While it reads like a Shakespearean tragedy, with the hero inexorably moving to his death, *The Gospel According to RFK* is of course modeled as well on the Gospels, which really are also the story of a man opening his eyes and ears, thinking and feeling, walking around, talking, as he forms the Christian idea of redemption, and of course also moves inexorably to his death. To preserve this itinerary of illumination in life and resolution in death, I have kept the order of the speeches, from March 16, when RFK announced for the presidency, to June 4, when he was fatally shot. Tragedy and redemption come together in the two stories of Jesus and RFK. In RFK's case it is the redemption of the American nation, the national vision of justice, freedom, and equality. The tragedy is that assassination, the ultimate censorship, silenced him. But the redemption is lost if his ideas are lost.

A great problem of modern life, it seems to me, has been the lack of systems of morality and ethics that can equal those of religions. Thus, modern, university-educated people may feel liberated from the constraints and superstitions of religions, but because of this they are also free from feeling obligated to contribute to their communities, help the poor, and work for peace. Works like *The Gospel According to RFK* can serve as secular ethical texts, encouraging the nonreligious and religious alike to assume some of the moral responsibility for the world around them.

I would like to acknowledge as inspiration for this book two works. Thomas Jefferson's edition of the Gospels removes those aspects of the text that rely upon faith (miracles, resurrection) and retains the story of the birth, life, ideas, and death of a man who lifted up the poor and praised the peacemakers.[11] *The Gospel According to Saint Matthew,* a film made in 1964 by Pier Paolo Pasolini, tells the story of Jesus and his ideas using the poorest of the poor of Southern Italian villages as his actors.[12]

I am glad that these texts are now available to the public; most were never before published in book form until the first edition of this book. In the John Fitzgerald Kennedy Library in Boston, there are many more speeches from RFK's entire career from 1955 to the end of the campaign. Some were published in 1993 in *RFK:*

Collected Speeches, edited by Edwin O. Guthman and C. Richard Allen.[13]

It is now the fortieth anniversary of Robert Kennedy's presidential campaign, and this new edition of *The Gospel According to RFK* marks that occasion. But in late November 2005, there was another celebration, for what would have been Bobby's eightieth birthday, in the Mike Mansfield Room at the U.S. Capitol, with his widow, Ethel, the honored guest. Speakers included his daughter Kerry Kennedy, his brother, Edward Kennedy, Harry Belafonte, Hillary Clinton, Barack Obama, John Kerry, Nancy Pelosi, Dennis Kucinich, John Lewis, Edward Markey, Mel Watts, Hilda Solis, Dolores Huerta, Jeff Greenfield, Father Robert Drinan, Rabbi Michael Lerner, and others. There was even a Republican, the MSNBC political commentator and former Congressman Joe Scarborough, who said, "[Robert Kennedy's] campaign did not end in Los Angeles. It continues to this day, if only those who have the ears to hear will take up the call, regardless of their party affiliation." Because Robert Kennedy read and loved poetry, I wrote a poem for him the night before in New York and read it that day at the Capitol.

For Robert Kennedy's 80th Birthday Celebration

*I write this in Bush's America
of torturing, Bush lying us to
war, Bush laughing at
the gap between the rich
and poor increasing.*

No one knows what you
would be like today.
I am not a mathematician
so have no equations
to bring you to 80
and tell us what you
and the world would be
like had you lived.

Thanksgiving 1967:
I came to New York
alone to live my life
with you as my senator
and I hoped my president.

June 1968: I had no TV,
was writing poetry about
Vietnam, went to bed for
a restless night, dreaming of
anguished voices in subway tunnels
beneath Astro Place and woke to
a beautiful morning and
moaning in the streets and shops.
You were dying. The line was a mile
long for your Saint Pat's requiem.

*Alone in an East Village room
that fall I wrote the words
"nostalgia for the future,"
not quite realizing
they were for you.*

*Your words and thoughts that year
kept you alive these years.
You became the president
of the other America
that we have carried around
thirty-seven years. You became
the president of this other America
that we salute today, where
everyone has a job and some hope,
where there is but one class,
where we honor the arts of
"mercy, pity, peace and love."*

*Peace to you, "warring soul
with your delicate anger."
Peace to our bloody world!*[14]

As I came to the last four lines, emotions overwhelmed me at the thought of all the horrors that have come about since the death of Robert Kennedy. Almost forty years of war and poverty, war against the poor, the hundreds of millions who have died because of lack of opportunity, lack of basic needs, lack of "mercy, pity, peace and love," to use William Blake's words. To say the last line, "Peace to our bloody world!" I had only one option: to spit it out.

Robert Kennedy believed that politics was an honorable profession, and that government could be used for the good of mankind. These speeches from his campaign forty years ago, these his last words before he was silenced, can be read today as an essential document of democratic humanity. I offer them in that spirit. They are words a man died for.

Norman MacAfee
New York City
January 1, 2008

1

"These are not ordinary times and this is not an ordinary election"

"Robert Francis Kennedy announced for President on My Lai morn."

—EDWARD SANDERS,
1968: A HISTORY IN VERSE[1]

ROBERT FRANCIS KENNEDY was President John Fitzgerald Kennedy's closest adviser and friend. As the attorney general from 1961 to 1964, RFK was the administration's enforcement arm for expanding civil rights into the South. He was also, notably, the crucial voice for reason and negotiation during perhaps the most perilous event in human history—the Cuban missile crisis of October 1962, when the United States and the Soviet Union came close to unleashing nuclear destruction on the Northern Hemisphere.[2]

In the later part of JFK's administration, his vice president, the Texan Lyndon Baines Johnson, increasingly felt marginalized among all the Harvard men, Bostonians, and other Northeasterners in the Kennedy circle. After JFK's assassination in Dallas on November 22, 1963, Johnson began to try to make his own mark as president, and Robert Kennedy soon found himself marginalized.

Of course, the worst of it for Bobby was that he had lost his brother. In the months following the assassination, he withdrew into himself, and read and reread the Greek classics and works by Albert Camus, trying to understand and perhaps accept what suffering means, and what it means to be human.

As the months passed after November 1963, it was generally assumed that RFK would run for the presidency, probably in 1972, since Johnson would be surely reelected in 1968. There was a sense that the country knew RFK better than any other politician because it had known his brother—that the values of the older brother would be carried on by the younger.

In 1964, RFK ran for and won a Senate seat representing New York. As the Vietnam war escalated under President Johnson through 1965 and 1966, the antiwar movement grew and Kennedy's private disagreement with Johnson's war policy became public. Most of those in the movement were Democrats who were urging RFK to oppose Johnson for the presidency. Kennedy was torn. He was against the war but felt that his running against Johnson in the primaries would be interpreted as a personal vendetta, and would divide the party and give the fall election to the Republicans. But he often quoted Dante: *The hottest places in hell are reserved for those who in times of moral crisis preserve their neutrality.* And 1967 was a time of the highest moral crisis and so a season in hell for RFK.

In early 1967, Barbara Garson's *MacBird!*, an off-Broadway satire inspired by *Macbeth*, summed up the situation. MacBird, Garson's version of LBJ, kills the king of Scotland, John Ken O'Dunc, and usurps the throne. In the final scene, MacBird, harried by guilt, is cornered by the surviving brother, Robert Ken O'Dunc. Robert raises his spear to kill his brother's assassin, but MacBird has a heart attack and dies, and Robert becomes king. It was a shadow play of the reality of the national political drama. In fact, Johnson would survive Bobby, but die of a heart attack a few years later.[3]

By late 1967, Kennedy still could not decide whether to run. The antiwar forces needed a presidential candidate, and Minnesota Senator Eugene McCarthy offered himself and soon dominated the movement. RFK went into a tormented eclipse, feeling that only he, and not McCarthy, whom he considered unambitious and cold in temperament, could beat Johnson, yet he was still unable to act.

At the end of January 1968, during the lunar new year, or Tet, the North Vietnamese and Viet Cong attacked thirty-six of forty-four South Vietnamese provincial capitals and invaded the U.S. Embassy in Saigon. The policies of the Johnson administration, which had been promising "light at the end of the tunnel" for years, suddenly were exposed as disastrously flawed, and public support for the war began collapsing.

In 1968's New Hampshire primary, McCarthy came in a close second to Johnson but won the most delegates to the convention. It was a huge victory for the antiwar movement. And now, because McCarthy had broken the ground, if Kennedy entered the race, it was less likely that he would be viewed as conducting the vendetta against LBJ.

On March 16, unknown to RFK, American soldiers massacred 500 unarmed civilians in the South Vietnamese hamlet of

My Lai. "Elderly people, women, young boys and girls, and babies were systematically shot while some of the troops refused to participate. One soldier missed a baby on the ground in front of him two times with a .45-caliber pistol before he finally hit his target, while his comrades laughed at what a bad shot he was."[4]

That day, in Washington, Kennedy announced his candidacy.

SENATE CAUCUS ROOM, SENATE OFFICE BUILDING
Washington, D.C., March 16, 1968

I am announcing today my candidacy for the Presidency of the United States.

I do not run for the Presidency merely to oppose any man but to propose new policies. I run because I am convinced that this country is on a perilous course and because I have such strong feelings about what must be done that I feel I am obliged to do all I can. I run to seek new policies—policies to close the gaps between black and white, rich and poor, young and old, in this country and around the world. I run for the presidency because I want the Democratic Party and the United States of America to stand for hope instead of despair, for reconciliation of men instead of the growing risk of world war.

I run because it is now unmistakably clear that we can change these disastrous, divisive policies only by changing the men who make them. . . .

No one who knows what I know about the extraordinary demands of the Presidency can be certain that any mortal can adequately fill it. But my service on the National Security Council during the Cuban Missile Crisis, the Berlin crisis of 1961 and 1962, and the negotiations on Laos and on the Nuclear Test Ban Treaty have taught me something about both the uses and limitations of military power, about the opportunities and the dangers which await our nation in the many corners of the globe to which I have traveled. As a member of the Cabinet and member of the Senate I have seen the inexcusable and ugly deprivation which causes children to starve in Mississippi, black citizens to riot in Watts, young Indians to commit suicide on their reservations, and proud and able-bodied families to wait out their lives in empty idleness in eastern Kentucky. I have talked and I have listened to the young people of our nation and felt their anger about the war that they are sent to fight and about the world they are about to inherit. In private talks and in public, I have tried in vain to alter our course in Vietnam before it further saps our spirit and our manpower, further raises the risks of wider war, and further destroys the country and the people it was meant to save.

I cannot stand aside from the contest that will decide our nation's future. The remarkable New Hampshire campaign of Senator Eugene McCarthy has proven how deep are the present divisions within our party and country. Until that was publicly clear, my presence in the race would have been seen as a clash of personalities rather than issues. But now that the fight is on over policies which I have long been challenging, I must enter that race. The fight is just beginning and I believe that I can win.

I have previously communicated this decision to President Johnson; and late last night, my brother, Senator Edward Kennedy, travelled to Wisconsin to communicate my decision to Senator McCarthy. I made clear to Senator McCarthy that my candidacy would not be in opposition to his, but in harmony. My aim is to both support and expand his valiant campaign in the spirit of his November 30th statement. Taking one month at a time, it is important that he achieve the largest possible majorities next month in the Wisconsin, Pennsylvania, and Massachusetts primaries. I strongly support his effort in those states and urge all my friends to give him their votes. Both of us will be encouraging like-minded Democrats in every state to select like-minded delegates to the National Convention—for both of us want above all else an open Democratic Convention at Chicago, free to choose a new course for our party and country. . . .

Finally, my decision reflects no personal animosity or disrespect toward President Johnson. He served President Kennedy with the utmost loyalty and was extremely kind to me and members of my family in the difficult months which followed the events of November, 1963. I have often commended his efforts in health, in education, and many other areas; and I have the deepest sympathy for the burden that he carries today. But the issue is not personal; it is our profound differences over where we are heading.

I do not lightly dismiss the dangers and difficulties of challenging an incumbent President; but these are not ordinary times and this is not an ordinary election. At stake is not simply the leadership of our party or even our country—it is our right to the moral leadership on this planet.

2

Ending the War

IN THE 1960s, there were no personal computers, cell phones, cable TV, 24-hour news channels, or blogs. Until the late summer of 1963, when CBS News, with anchor Walter Cronkite, broadcast the first half-hour nightly news show, the networks devoted only fifteen minutes each evening to national and world news. That inaugural show included an interview with President Kennedy famously saying of the South Vietnamese, "In the final analysis, it is *their* war." There were at that time 16,000 U.S. advisers in Vietnam. In the next years, especially from 1965 on, Americans began seeing stories and images of death and destruction on their half-hour nightly news shows. By early 1968, there were 600,000 American soldiers in Vietnam, and 19,000 had died. It was becoming a war that fewer and fewer could stomach.

In February 1968, Cronkite went to Vietnam to see firsthand the progress of the war. In a February 27, 1968, broadcast, he concluded that the war was a quagmire, and the only honorable way to end it was through honest negotiations. By this time, Cronkite was one of the most respected figures in the country, and more than 9 million people watched his report and took his remarks to heart.[1]

The day after Robert Kennedy announced his candidacy, he marched in the St. Patrick's Day parades in Boston and New York, then—with his wife, Ethel, and his entourage—flew to Kansas. RFK was identified with big northeastern cities and liberal politics, while Kansas is a largely rural, mostly white, conservative midwestern state, so he was surprised by the large and friendly crowds. His first speech, delivered to 14,500 students and faculty at Kansas State University's fieldhouse, concentrated on the reasons he opposed the Vietnam war.

The response to the hour-long speech was ecstatic: "The fieldhouse sounded as though it was inside Niagara Falls. . . . The sound of screaming filled the fieldhouse, and hundreds of students were running toward the platform, overturning chairs, raising a haze of dust from the dirt floor. They surrounded him, screamed his name, pulled his cuff links, scratched his hands."[2] The response to RFK among the young fit in with the times. In 1968, what was being called the counterculture was in full bloom. As young men were drafted, long-haired hippies were putting flowers in the barrels of soldiers' rifles, "Make Love Not War" their mantra. Bobby—with his long hair and rumpled suit and tie—could be said to be at the establishment end of the counterculture. "I'm a Beatle," he joked.

I include most of this quite long and extraordinary speech not just because it was the first speech of the campaign, but because it set out solutions to the one problem, the war, that stood in the way of solutions to all the other problems the country faced. In our times, the Iraq war can be compared to the Vietnam war, consuming the national treasury and destroying the national sense of progress and idealism. When RFK says that American policy is "creating more Viet Cong than we are destroying," he could be talking about Iraq's insurgents and so-called terrorists. One can imagine how RFK would have reacted to the invasion of Iraq based on this and other speeches. But there is further evidence: His younger brother, Senator Edward Kennedy, thirty-six in 1968 but now a Democratic elder statesman, has been a scathing critic of Bush's war. "There was no imminent threat," he said in September 2003. "This was made up in Texas, announced in January to the Republican leadership that war was going to take place and was going to be good politically. This whole thing was a fraud."[3]

But there are differences between the two times and the two wars. North Vietnam's Ho Chi Minh was seen by most of the world as a freedom fighter strongly influenced by the American Revolution and the founders of the Republic. Saddam Hussein was widely conceded to have been a corrupt despot guilty of mass torture and murder, though, ironically, he was heartily supported and heavily armed by the administrations of Ronald Reagan and the first Bush from 1981 to 1990, during which most of the mass murder took place. Lyndon Johnson at least balanced his disastrous war in Vietnam with his Great Society, War on Poverty, and civil rights programs, which tried to help the majority of his fellow citizens. George W. Bush's policies had no such balance. His war, ostensibly waged to destroy Iraq's nonexistent weapons of mass destruction and avenge Saddam Hussein's nonexistent link to the 9/11 attacks, seems to have been started for a number of other, less overt, reasons—access to oil, contracts for corrupt Bush cronies like Dick Cheney's Halliburton, and reelection through the blackmailing tactic of sending and keeping American troops in harm's way. The Iraq war was accompanied by tax cuts that benefit only the wealthiest and devastate government services to the average American. From Johnson, a War on Poverty; from Bush, a war to make more and more Americans poor.

KANSAS STATE UNIVERSITY
Manhattan, Kansas, March 18, 1968, 10:00 a.m.

. . . I come here, to this serious forum in the heart of the nation, to discuss this war with you; not on the basis of emotion, but fact; not, I hope, in clichés, but with a clear and discriminating sense of where the national interest really lies.

I do not want—as I believe most Americans do not want—to sell out American interests, to simply withdraw, to raise the white flag of surrender. That would be unacceptable to us as a country and as a people. But, I am concerned—as I believe most Americans are concerned—that the course we are following at the present time is deeply wrong. I am concerned—as I believe most Americans are concerned—that we are acting as if no other nations existed, against the judgment and desires of neutrals and our historic allies alike. I am concerned—as I believe most Americans are concerned—that our present course will not bring victory; will not bring peace; will not stop the bloodshed; and will not advance the interests of the United States or the cause of peace in the world.

I am concerned that, at the end of it all, there will only be more Americans killed; more of our treasure spilled out; and because of the bitterness and hatred on every side of this war, more hundreds of thousands of Vietnamese slaughtered; so that they may say, as Tacitus said of Rome: "They made a desert, and called it peace."

And I do not think that is what the American spirit is really all about.

Let me begin this discussion with a note both personal and public. I was involved in many of the early decisions of Vietnam, decisions which helped set us on our present path. It may be that the effort was doomed from the start; that it was never really possible to bring all the people of South Vietnam under the rule of the successive governments we supported—governments, one after another, riddled with corruption, inefficiency, and greed; governments which did not and could not successfully capture and energize the national feeling of their people. If that is the case, as it well may be, then I am willing to bear my share of the responsibility, before history and before my fellow-citizens. But past error is no excuse for its own perpetuation. . . .

The reversals of the last several months have led our military to ask for 206,000 more troops. This weekend, it was announced that some of them—a "moderate" increase, it was said—would soon be sent. But isn't this exactly what we have always done in the past? If we examine the history of this conflict, we find the dismal story repeated time after time. Every time—at every crisis—we have denied that anything was wrong; sent more troops; and issued more confident communiqués. Every time, we have been assured that this one last step would bring victory. And every time, the predictions and promises have failed and been forgotten, and the demand has been made again for just one more step up the ladder.

But all the escalations, all the last steps, have brought us no closer to success than we were before. Rather, as the scale of the fighting has increased, South Vietnamese society has become less and less capable of organizing or defending itself, and we have more and more assumed the whole burden of the war. In just three years, we have gone from 16,000 advisers to over 600,000 troops; from no American bombing North or South, to an air campaign against both, greater than that waged in all the European theater in World War II; from less than 300 American dead in all the years prior to 1965, to more than 500 dead in a single week of combat in 1968—509 this very week.

And once again, the President tells us, as we have been told for twenty years, that "we are going to win"; "victory" is coming.

But what are the true facts? What is our present situation?

First, our control over the rural population—so long described as the key to our efforts—has evaporated. The Vice President [Hubert Humphrey] tells us that the pacification program has "stopped." In the language of other high officials, it is a "considerable setback," with "loss of momentum," "some withdrawal from the countryside," "a significant psychological setback on the part of pacification people themselves and the local population." Reports from the field indicate that the South Vietnamese Army has greatly increased its tendency "to pull into its compounds in cities and towns, especially at night, reduce its patrolling, and leave the militia and revolutionary development cadres open to enemy incursion and attack." Undoubtedly, this is one reason why, over the last two weeks, our combat deaths—1049—were so much greater than those of the South Vietnamese—557. Like it or not, the government of South Vietnam is pursuing an enclave policy. Its writ runs where American arms protect it: that far and no farther. To extend the power of the Saigon government over its own country, we now can see, will be in essence equivalent to the reconquest and occupation of most of the entire nation.

Let us clearly understand the full implications of that fact. The point of our pacification operations was always described as "winning the hearts and minds" of the people. We recognized that giving the countryside military security against the Viet Cong would be futile—indeed that it would be impossible—unless the people of the countryside themselves came to identify their interests with ours, and to assist not the Viet Cong but the Saigon government. For this we recognized that their minds would have to be *changed*—that their natural inclination would be to support the Viet Cong, or at best remain passive, rather than sacrifice for foreign white men, or the remote Saigon government.

It is this effort that has been most gravely set back in the last month. We cannot change the minds of the people in villages controlled by the enemy. The fact is, as all recognize, that we cannot reassert control of those villages now in enemy hands without repeating the whole process of bloody destruction which has ravaged the countryside of South Vietnam throughout the last three years. Nor could we thus keep control without the presence of millions of American troops. If, in the years those villages and hamlets were controlled by Saigon, the government had brought honesty, social reform, land—if that had happened, if the many promises of a new and better life for the people had been fulfilled—then, in the process of reconquest, we might appear as liberators: just as we did in Europe, despite the devastation of war, in 1944–45. But the promises of reform were not kept. Corruption and abuse of administrative power have continued to this day. Land reform has never been more than an empty promise. Viewing the performance of the Saigon government over the last three years, there is no reason for the South Vietnamese peasant to fight for the extension of its authority or to view the further devastation that effort will bring as anything but a calamity. Yet already the destruction has defeated most of our own purposes. Arthur Gardiner is the former chief of the United States AID mission in South Vietnam, and currently Executive Director of the International Voluntary Services. He tells us that we are "creating more Viet Cong than we are destroying"—and "increasing numbers of Vietnamese are becoming benevolently neutral toward the Viet Cong." As a consequence, the political war—so long described as the only war that counts—has gone with the pacification program that was to win it. In a real sense, it may now be lost beyond recall.

The second evident fact of the last two months is that the Saigon government is no more or better an ally than it was before; that it may even be less; and that the war inexorably is growing more, not less, an American effort. American officials continue to talk about a government newly energized, moving with "great competence," taking hold "remarkably well," doing "a very, very good piece of work of recovery." I was in the Executive Branch of the government from 1961 to 1964. In all those years, we heard the same glowing promises about the South Vietnamese government: corruption would soon be eliminated, land reform would come, programs were being infused with new energy. But those were not the facts then, and they are not the facts today. The facts are that there is still no total mobilization: no price or wage controls, no rationing, no overtime work. The facts are, as a Committee of the House of Representatives has told us, that land reform is moving backward, with the government forces helping landlords to collect exorbitant back rents from the peasantry. The facts are that 18-year-old South Vietnamese are still not being drafted; though now, as many times in the past, we are assured that this will happen soon. The facts are that thousands of young South Vietnamese buy their deferments from military service while American Marines die at Khe Sanh.

The facts are that the government has arrested monks and labor leaders, former Presidential candidates and government officials—including prominent members of the Committee for the Preservation of the Nation, in which American officials placed such high hopes just a few weeks ago.

Meanwhile, the government's enormous corruption continues, debilitating South Vietnam and crippling our effort to help its people. Committees of the Senate and House of Representatives have officially documented the existence, extent, and results of this corruption: American AID money stolen, food diverted from refugees, government posts bought and sold while essential tasks remain undone. A subcommittee of the Senate Committee on Government Operations has reported that the Vietnamese Collector of Customs had engaged in smuggling gold and opium—and that he was protected by figures even higher in the government. President Johnson has responded to corruption in Vietnam by reminding us that there is stealing in Beaumont, Texas. I for one do not believe that Beaumont is so corrupt. I do not believe that any public official, in any American city, is engaged in smuggling gold and dope, selling draft deferments, or pocketing millions of dollars in U.S. government funds. But however corrupt any city in the United States may be, that corruption is not costing the lives of American soldiers; while the pervasive corruption of the Government of Vietnam, as an American official has told us, is a significant cause *of* the prolongation of the war and the continued American casualties. As this government continues on its present course, and our support for it continues, the effect can only be to leave us totally isolated from the people of Vietnam. Our fighting men deserve better than that.

Third, it is becoming more evident with every passing day that the victories we achieve will only come at the cost of destruction for the nation we once hoped to help. Even before this winter, Vietnam and its people were disintegrating under the blows of war. Now hardly a city in Vietnam has been spared from the new ravages of the past two months. Saigon officials say that nearly three quarters of a million new refugees have been created, to add to the existing refugee population of two million or more. No one really knows the number of civilian casualties. The city of Hue, with most of the country's cultural and artistic heritage, lies in ruins: Of its population of 145,000, fully 113,000 are said to be homeless. There is not enough food, not enough shelter, not enough medical care. There is only death and misery and destruction.

An American commander said of the town of Ben Tre, "it became necessary to destroy the town in order to save it." It is difficult to quarrel with the decision of American commanders to use air power and artillery to save the lives of their men; if American troops are to fight for Vietnamese cities, they deserve protection. What I cannot understand is why the responsibility for the recapture and attendant destruction of Hue, and Ben Tre and the others, should fall to American troops in the first place.

If Communist insurgents or invaders held New York or Washington or San Francisco, we would not leave it to foreigners to take them back, and destroy them and their people in the process. Rather I believe there is not one among us who would not tear the invaders out with his bare hands, whatever the cost. There is no question that some of the South Vietnamese Army fought with great bravery. The Vietnamese—as these units and the Viet Cong have both shown us—are a courageous people. But it is also true that a thousand South Vietnamese soldiers, in Hue on leave for Tet, hid among the refugees for three weeks, making no attempt to rejoin their units or join the town's defense; among them was a full colonel. And it is also true that in the height of the battle for Hue, as trucks brought back American dead and wounded from the front lines, millions of Americans could see, on their television screens, South Vietnamese soldiers occupied in looting the city those Americans were fighting to recapture.

If the government's troops will not or cannot carry the fight for their cities, we cannot ourselves destroy them. That kind of salvation is not an act we can presume to perform for them. For we must ask our government—we must ask ourselves: where does such logic end? If it becomes "necessary" to destroy all of South Vietnam in order to "save" it, will we do that too? And if we care so little about South Vietnam that we are willing to see the land destroyed and its people dead, then why are we there in the first place?

Can we ordain to ourselves the awful majesty of God—to decide what cities and villages are to be destroyed, who will live and who will die, and who will join the refugees wandering in a desert of our own creation? . . .

Let us have no misunderstanding. The Viet Cong are a brutal enemy indeed. Time and time again, they have shown their willingness to sacrifice innocent civilians, to engage in torture and murder and despicable terror to achieve their ends. This is a war almost without rules or quarter. There can be no easy moral answer to this war, no one-sided condemnation of American actions. What we must ask ourselves is whether we have a right to bring so much destruction to another land without clear and convincing evidence that this is what its people want. But that is precisely the evidence we do not have. What they want is peace, not dominated by any outside forces. And that is what we are really committed to help bring them, not in some indefinite future, but while some scraps of life remain still to be saved from the holocaust.

The fourth fact that is now more clear than ever is that the war in Vietnam, far from being the last critical test for the United States, is in fact weakening our position in Asia and around the world, and eroding the structure of international cooperation which has directly supported our security for the past three decades. In purely military terms, the war has already stripped us of the graduated-response capability that we have labored so hard to build for the last seven years. Surely the North Koreans were emboldened to seize the *Pueblo* because they knew that the United States simply cannot afford to fight another Asian war while we are so tied down in Vietnam. We set out to prove our willingness to keep our commitments everywhere in the world. What we are ensuring instead is that it is most unlikely that the American people would ever again be willing to again engage in this kind of struggle. Meanwhile our oldest and strongest allies pull back to their own shores, leaving us alone to police all of Asia. . . .

All this bears directly and heavily on the questions of whether more troops should now be sent to Vietnam—and, if more are sent, what their mission will be. We will be entitled to ask—we are required to ask—how many more men, how many more lives, how much more destruction will be asked, to provide the military victory that is always just around the corner, to pour into this bottomless pit of our dreams?

But this question the Administration does not and cannot answer. It has no answer—none but the ever-expanding use of military force and the lives of our brave soldiers, in a conflict where military force has failed to solve anything in the past. The President has offered to negotiate—yet this weekend he told us again that he seeks not compromise but victory, "at the negotiating table, if possible, on the battlefield if necessary." But at a real negotiating table, there can be no "victory" for either side; only a painful and difficult compromise. To seek victory at the conference table is to ensure that you will never reach it. Instead the war will go on, year after terrible year—until those who sit in the seats of high policy are men who seek another path. And that must be done this year.

For it is long past time to ask: what is this war doing to us? Of course it is costing us money—fully one-fourth of our federal budget—but that is the smallest price we pay. The cost is in our young men, the tens of thousands of their lives cut off forever. The cost is in our world position—in neutrals and allies alike, every day more baffled by and estranged from a policy they cannot understand.

Higher yet is the price we pay in our own innermost lives, and in the spirit of our country. For the first time in a century, we have open resistance to service in the cause of the nation. For the first time perhaps in our history, we have desertions from our army on political and moral grounds. The front pages of our newspapers show photographs of American soldiers torturing prisoners. Every night we watch horrors on the evening news. Violence spreads inexorably across the nation, filling our streets and crippling our lives. And whatever the costs to us, let us think of the young men we have sent there: not just the killed, but those who have to kill; not just the maimed, but also those who must look upon the results of what they do.

It may be asked: Is not such degradation the cost of all wars? Of course it is. That is why war is not an enterprise lightly to be undertaken, nor prolonged one moment past its absolute necessity. All this—the destruction of Vietnam, the cost to ourselves, the danger to the world—all this we would stand, willingly, if it seemed to serve some worthwhile end. But the costs of the war's present course far outweigh anything we can reasonably hope to gain by it, for ourselves or for the people of Vietnam. It must be ended, and it can be ended in a peace for brave men who have fought each other with a terrible fury, each believing that he alone was in the right. We have prayed to different gods, and the prayers of neither have been answered fully. Now, while there is still time for some of them to be partly answered, now is the time to stop.

And the fact is that much can be done. We can—as I have urged for two years, but as we have never done—negotiate with the National Liberation Front. We can—as we have never done—assure the Front a genuine place in the political life of South Vietnam. We can—as we are refusing to do today—begin to deescalate the war, concentrate on protecting populated areas, and thus save American lives and slow down the destruction of the countryside. We can—as we have never done—insist that the Government of South Vietnam broaden its base, institute real reforms, and seek an honorable settlement with their fellow countrymen.

This is no radical program of surrender. This is no sell-out of American interests. This is a modest and reasonable program, designed to advance the interests of this country and save something from the wreckage for the people of Vietnam.

This program would be far more effective than the present course of this Administration—whose only response to failure is to repeat it on a larger scale. This program, with its more limited costs, would indeed be far more likely to accomplish our true objectives.

And therefore even this modest and reasonable program is impossible while our present leadership, under the illusion that military victory is just ahead, plunges deeper into the swamp that is our present course.

So I come here today, to this great University, to ask your help: not for me, but for your country and for the people of Vietnam. You are the people, as President Kennedy said, who have "the least ties to the present and the greatest ties to the future." I urge you to learn the harsh facts that lurk behind the mask of official illusion with which we have concealed our true circumstances, even from ourselves. Our country is in danger: not just from foreign enemies; but above all, from our own misguided policies—

and what they can do to the nation that Thomas Jefferson once told us was the last, best, hope of man. There is a contest on, not for the rule of America, but for the heart of America. In these next eight months, we are going to decide what this country will stand for—and what kind of men we are. So I ask for your help, in the cities and homes of this state, in the towns and farms: contributing your concern and action, warning of the danger of what we are doing—and the promise of what we can do. I ask you, as tens of thousands of young men and women are doing all over this land, to organize yourselves, and then to go forth and work for new policies—work to change our direction—and thus restore our place at the point of moral leadership, in our country, in our own hearts, and all around the world.

The Other America

Robert Kennedy's bond with the poor and hungry seemed total. It came from a childhood identification with the underdog and grew when he visited urban ghettoes and Native American reservations. He went to the Mississippi Delta in the spring of 1967 to see firsthand the effects of child hunger and encountered children who had "swollen bellies and running sores on their arms and legs that appeared not to be healing" and who ate only once a day. Later, back in Washington, RFK told the secretary of agriculture, Orville Freeman, what he'd seen. The secretary found it hard to believe that there were still Americans who were literally dying of hunger, but after he'd looked into it, Freeman immediately changed the food stamp policy to alleviate the problem.[1]

There is another clue as to why RFK cared so much for the poor. Going through his brother's papers after the assassination, he came upon "a scrap of paper from President Kennedy's last cabinet meeting," writes Evan Thomas. "On it, the president had scribbled the word 'poverty' several times and circled it. . . . To RFK, the mere mention of the word 'poverty' was a kind of last testament. He had the scrap of paper framed and kept on display at his office."[2]

RFK's first Kansas speech, in the morning of March 18, 1968, concentrated on the war in Vietnam. That afternoon, at another campus in Kansas, he repeated much of that speech but added material about the problems of poverty.

According to Jack Newfield, a few weeks later at a dinner with friends, RFK said something, a very simple idea, that illuminates his entire campaign and his thought: "It's class, not color. What everyone wants is a job and some hope."[3]

Since 1968, the gap between rich and poor has widened year by year until it is now a vast chasm. Economist Paul Krugman supplies figures from 1979 to 1997, from the Carter administration through twelve years of two Republican presidents and into the fifth year of the Clinton administration: "adjusting for inflation, the income of families in the middle of the U.S. income distribution rose from $41,400 in 1979, to $45,100 in 1997, a 9 percent increase. Meanwhile the income of families in the top 1 percent rose from $420,200 to $1.1016 million, a 160 percent increase. Or to put it another way, the income of families in the top 1 percent was 10 times that of typical families in 1979 and 23 times and rising in 1997."[4] Writing in 2006, Democratic Senator James Webb of Virginia noted the accelerating gap in the average salaries of workers and the heads of their companies: In the 1960s, the ratio was 20 to 1; by the year 2000, it was 400 to 1.[5]

UNIVERSITY OF KANSAS
Lawrence, Kansas, March 18, 1968, Afternoon

For we as a people are strong enough, we are brave enough to be told the truth of where we stand. And this country needs honesty and candor in its political life and from the President of the United States. But I don't want to run for the presidency, I don't want America to make the critical choice of direction and leadership this year without confronting that truth. I don't want to win the support of those by hiding the American condition in false hopes or illusions. I want us to find out the promise of the future, what we *can* accomplish here in the United States, what this country *does* stand for, and what is expected of us in the years ahead. And I also want us to know and examine where we've gone wrong. And I want all of us, young and old, to have a chance to build a better country and change the direction of the United States of America.

This morning I spoke about the war in Vietnam and I will speak briefly about it in a few moments. But there is much more to this critical election year than the war in Vietnam. It is at root, the root of all of it, the national soul of the United States. The president calls it restlessness. Our cabinet officers such as John Gardner and others tell us that America is in a deep malaise of spirit, discouraging initiative, paralyzing will and action, and dividing Americans from one another by their age, their views, and by the color of their skin, and I don't think we have to accept that in the United States of America. Demonstrators shout down government officials, and the government answers by drafting demonstrators. Anarchists threaten to burn the country down, and some have begun to try while tanks patrol American streets and machine guns have fired at American children. I don't think this is a satisfactory situation for the United States of America. Our young people, the best educated and the best comforted in our history, turn from the Peace Corps and public commitment of a few years ago to lives of disengagement and despair, many of them turned on with drugs and turned off with America. (None of them, of course, here in Kansas. Right?) All around us, not just on the question of Vietnam, not just on the question of the cities, not just on the question of the poverty, not just on the problem of the race relations, but all around us, and why *you* are so concerned, the fact is that men have lost confidence in themselves, in each other, confidence which has sustained us so much in the past. Rather than answer the cries of deprivation and despair, cries which the President's Commission on Civil Disorders tells us could finally split our nation asunder, rather than answer these desperate cries, hundreds of communities and millions of citizens are looking for their answers through force and repression and private gun stocks, so that we confront our fellow citizens across impassable barriers of hostility and mistrust and again I don't believe that we have to accept that, I don't believe that it is necessary in the United States of America, I think that we can work together, I don't think that we have to shoot at each other, to beat each other, to curse each other and criticize each other. I think that we can do better in this country. And that is why I run for President of the United States. And if we seem powerless to stop this growing division between Americans who at least confront one another, there are millions more living in the hidden places whose names and faces are completely unknown.

But I have seen these other Americans—I have seen children in Mississippi starving, their bodies so crippled by hunger: and their minds have been so destroyed for their whole life that they will have no future. I have seen children in Mississippi—here in the United States, with a gross national product of eight hundred billion dollars—I have seen children in the Delta area of Mississippi with distended stomachs, whose faces are covered with sores from starvation, and we haven't developed a policy so that we can get enough food so that they can live, so that their lives are not destroyed. I don't think that's acceptable in the United States of America and I think we need a change.

I have seen Indians living on their bare and meager reservations, with no jobs, with an unemployment rate of 80 percent, and with so little hope for the future that for young people, young men and women in their teens, the greatest cause of death is suicide, that they end their lives by killing themselves—I don't think that we have to accept that, for the first Americans, for the minority here in the United States. If young boys and girls are so filled with despair when they are going to high school and feel that their lives are so hopeless and that nobody's going to care for them, nobody's going to be involved with them, nobody's going to bother with them, that they either hang themselves, shoot themselves, or kill themselves—I don't think that's acceptable and I think the United States of America, I think the American people, I think we can do much, much better. And I run for the presidency because of that. I run for the presidency because I have seen proud men in the hills of Appalachia, who wish only to work in dignity, but they cannot, for the mines are closed and their jobs are gone and no one, neither industry nor labor nor government, has cared enough to help.

I think we here in this country, with the unselfish state that exists in the United States of America, I think we can do better here also. I have seen the people of the black ghetto, listening to ever-greater promises of equality and of justice, as they sit in the same decaying schools and huddle in the same filthy rooms, without heat, warding off the cold and warding off the rats.

If we believe that we as Americans are bound together by a common concern for each other, then an urgent national priority is upon us. We must begin to end the disgrace of this other America. And this is one of the great tasks of leadership for us, as individuals and citizens this year.

But even if we act to erase material poverty, there is another greater task. It is to confront the poverty of satisfaction, purpose, and dignity that inflicts us all. Too much and too long, we seem to have surrendered community excellence and community values in the mere accumulation of material things. Our gross national product now is over eight hundred billion dollars a year, but that gross national product—if we should judge the United States of America by that—that gross national product counts air pollution and cigarette advertising and ambulances to clear our highways of carnage. It counts special locks for our doors and the jails for the people who break them. It counts the destruction of the redwoods and the loss of our natural wonder in chaotic sprawl. It counts napalm, and it counts nuclear warheads, and armored cars for the police to fight the riots in our cities. It counts . . . the television programs which glorify violence in order to sell toys to our children.

Yet the gross national product does not allow for the health of our children, the quality of their education, or the joy of their play. It does not include the beauty of our poetry or the strength of our marriages, the intelligence of our public debate or the integrity of our public officials. It measures neither our wit nor our courage; neither our wisdom nor our learning; neither our compassion nor our devotion to our country; it measures everything, in short, except that which makes life worthwhile, and it can tell us everything about America except why we are proud that we are Americans. If this is true here at home, so it is true elsewhere in the world. From the beginning, our proudest boast has been the promise of Jefferson, that we here in this country would be the best hope of mankind. And now as we look at the war in Vietnam, we wonder if we still hold a decent respect for the opinions of mankind and whether the opinion maintained a decent respect for us, or whether like Athens of old, we will forfeit sympathy and support and ultimately our very security in the single-minded pursuit of our own goals and our own objectives. . . .

4

Dissent in Time of War

IN THE FOLLOWING SPEECH, delivered at Vanderbilt University in Nashville, it is heartening to read RFK on the subject of dissent. Before 1968, there was a tradition of bipartisan foreign policy, of "politics stopping at the water's edge." But in the 1968 presidential race, too many people disagreed with Johnson's war to maintain the façade of consensus. During RFK's campaign, however, few of his fellow war critics in the Senate dared to support Kennedy, fearing retaliation by President Johnson. RFK's criticism of the war caused him to be accused of giving aid and comfort to the enemy, endangering the troops, even being a traitor.

In Nashville, RFK gave several defenses of dissent. Perhaps the most relevant to our time is the following: "debate is all we have to prevent past errors from leading us down the road to disaster. How else is error to be corrected, if not by the informed reason of dissent?"

Thirty-six years after RFK's speech in Nashville, former vice president Al Gore spoke at Vanderbilt in February 2004 and bravely accused Bush of deceiving the world about Saddam Hussein's weapons of mass destruction and links to 9/11. "He betrayed this country! He played on our fears. He took America on an ill-conceived foreign adventure dangerous to our troops, an adventure preordained and planned before 9/11 ever took place."[1]

Those who criticize the invasion of Iraq or the apparently never-ending "War on Terror" may be fearful of retaliation in the repressive atmosphere after 9/11 and the USA Patriot Act. But as RFK said in Nashville in similarly troubled times, "I urge you to learn the harsh facts that lurk behind the mask of official illusion with which we have concealed our true circumstances, even from ourselves. Our country is in danger: Not just from foreign enemies; but above all, from our own misguided policies, and what they can do to this country."

VANDERBILT UNIVERSITY
Nashville, Tennessee, March 21, 1968

. . . For generations, we have been struggling with the problems of race and discrimination. A few years ago, there were civil rights demonstrations, sit-ins, and marches, argument and discontent. But we were moving forward: cooperation and agreement were growing daily between black and white, North and South. Now anarchists threaten to burn the country down, and some have begun to try—while tanks have patrolled American streets and machine-guns have fired at American children. The President tells us that we can look forward to summer after summer of riot and repression. Here in Nashville, as all across the country, we have seen the tragic and intolerable consequences. I dissent from that, and I know you do too.

And there are other divisions, equally serious, tearing at the fabric of our national unity. Demonstrators shout down government officials, and the Selective Service silences protesters. Young people—the best educated in our history—turn from the Peace Corps and public commitment of a few years ago to lives of disengagement and despair, turning on with drugs, and turning off America. And that is something to dissent from.

So when we are told to forgo all dissent and division, we must ask: Who is it that is truly dividing the country? It is not those who call for change; it is those who make present policy who divide our country; those who bear the responsibility for our present course; those who have removed themselves from the American tradition, from the enduring and generous impulses that are the soul of the nation.

Those who now call for an end to dissent, moreover, seem not to understand what this country is all about. For debate and dissent are the very heart of the American process. We have followed the wisdom of Greece: "All things are to be examined and brought into question. There is no limit set to thought."

For debate is all we have to prevent past errors from leading us down the road to disaster. How else is error to be corrected, if not by the informed reason of dissent? Every dictatorship has ultimately strangled in the web of repression it wove for its people, making mistakes that could not be corrected because criticism was prohibited. . . .

A second purpose of debate is to give voice and recognition to those without the power to be heard. There are millions of Americans living in hidden places, whose faces and names we never know. But I have seen children starving in Mississippi, idling their lives away in the ghetto, living without hope or future amid the despair on Indian reservations, with no jobs and little hope. I have seen proud men in the hills of Appalachia, who wish only to work in dignity—but the mines are closed, and the jobs are gone and no one, neither industry or labor or government, has cared enough to help. Those conditions will change, those children will live, only if we dissent. So I dissent, and I know you do too.

A third reason for dissent is not because it is comforting, but because it is not—because it sharply reminds us of our basic ideals and true purpose. Only broad and fundamental dissent will allow us to confront—not only material poverty—but the poverty of satisfaction that afflicts us all. . . .

So if we are uneasy about our country today, perhaps it is because we are truer to our principles than we realize, because we know that our happiness will come not from goods we have, but from the good we do together.

And as this is true at home, so it is true in the world. From the beginning it was our proudest boast, as Jefferson said, that we were the "last best hope of mankind." Now we look at the war in Vietnam. . . . In what way does the war's present course advance the security of this country, the welfare of Vietnam, or the cause of peace in the world? We ask this, and say with Camus: "I should like to be able to love my country and still love justice." We know then that all this is our responsibility, yours and mine and millions like us, and that it is far too important a matter to be entrusted to remote generals and leaders. We sense that this is not what the American spirit is really about. So I dissent. And you dissent. We are going to turn this country around.

For that is, finally, the real destiny of dissent. It is to bring our differences forth, to confront each other with honesty and candor—and then, to look across the barriers which divide us, by our ages, our views, and the color of our skins—to look across these false barriers to the enduring and lasting impulses that have always united Americans in times of crisis: the faith that we as citizens can master and bring to our service the enormous forces that rage across the world we live in. . . .

≣ 5 ≣

National Reconciliation

A FEW HOURS AFTER his Nashville speech, RFK spoke in Alabama, where in 1963 as attorney general he had brought about the racial integration of the University of Alabama over the opposition of the governor, George Wallace. Kennedy had overseen much of the integration of the South, and to most African Americans, he was a hero; to many white Southerners, he symbolized a loss of their power.

Since the administration of Franklin Roosevelt, the South had voted overwhelmingly Democratic. But times were changing, and RFK's reception at the university he had helped integrate was merely cordial. In the general election of 1968, Wallace would run on a third-party ticket, taking votes that would normally have gone to the Democratic nominee, Hubert Humphrey, thus delivering the presidency to Richard Nixon.

The old questions of race continue to be used to divide Southerners not only from each other but also from the rest of the country. Republicans have increasingly won the Southern white vote by encouraging white prejudice against blacks. But Robert Kennedy's intuition that "It's class, not color" is essential to understanding the real dynamics of the economy and politics of the South as well as the nation. Genuine reconciliation can come about if we understand that, as RFK said, "What everyone wants is a job and some hope."

University of Alabama
Tuscaloosa, Alabama, March 21, 1968

. . . I have come here to Alabama to talk with you of the hope which binds us together as Americans; and to ask for your help.

For America's successes were not built by men of narrow region, refusing to look beyond their own sectional concerns. The settling of the prairie by men of the East, the fight to build the Tennessee Valley Authority, led by George Norris of Nebraska and Franklin D. Roosevelt of New York, the battle of Alabama's Hugo Black for the rights of labor and free speech—these are triumphs for a whole nation, made by men who were first, and always, Americans. This is the spirit in which I come to Alabama.

I have come here because our great nation is troubled, divided as never before in our history; divided by a difficult, costly war abroad and by bitter, destructive crisis at home; divided by our age, by our beliefs, by the color of our skins. I have come here because I seek to join with you in building a better country and a united country. And I come to Alabama because I need your help.

For this campaign, in this critical election year, must be far more than a matter of political organization, of courting and counting votes. This election will mean nothing if it leaves us, after it is all over, as divided as we were when it began. We have to begin to put our country together again. So I believe that any who seek high office this year must go before all Americans: not just those who agree with them, but also those who disagree; recognizing that it is not just our supporters, not just those who vote for us, but all Americans, who we must lead in the difficult years ahead. And this is why I have come, at the outset of my campaign, not to New York or Chicago or Boston: but here to Alabama.

Some have said there are many issues on which we disagree. For my part, I do not believe these disagreements are as great as the principles which unite us. And I also think we can confront those issues with candor and truth, and confront each other as men. We need not paper over our differences on specific issues— if we can, as we must, remember always our common burden and our common hope as Americans.

A few short years ago, Americans were divided over issues which seemed immense: whether a Negro citizen should attend school here at the University of Alabama; whether he should have the right to eat a meal in a public restaurant; whether he should have the right to vote.

But these quarrels are behind us now. . . .

For the work we must do is not for the benefit of any one of our peoples: It is work we must do for all Americans. The proud men of Eastern Kentucky, seeking work in dignity, finding only the insult of a welfare handout—these men are the brothers of our ghetto families. City slum and rural hollow alike, both live out their lives crowded into filthy rooms without jobs and without hope, surviving on the same welfare handouts, thrust at them by the same indifferent government. These men are united in deprivation with the youth of our Indian reservations and Mexican-American families and countless others.

All these Americans are joined by the bond of injustice—and all these Americans must be freed by a strong, determined national effort—not an effort which merely swells our budget with programs which will not free these Americans—but an effort which will provide jobs, not welfare doles; decent homes, not slums standing on the foundation of federal indifference.

This is the year when we can begin that effort. This is the year we can change the common sources of this suffering. This is the year when all of us—you and I—can put forth our convictions and our energy to the service of our country: we can turn away from separation. We can unite America. And I am here in Alabama to ask your help in this task.

For history has placed us all, Northerner and Southerner, black and white, within a common border and under a common law. All of us, from the wealthiest and most powerful of men, to the weakest and hungriest of children, share one precious possession: the name "American."

So I come to Alabama to ask you to help in the task of national reconciliation: to place your energies and your time and your strength in the first work of America: the building of a nation united not on every issue, but in the enduring faith that men are to be free—that men are to have the chance for a decent life—that the natural condition of man is not degradation, but dignity. . . .

6

California Rallies

IN CALIFORNIA, AS Kennedy threw himself into campaigning, he had good news: A Gallup poll of the nation's Democratic voters showed him beating Johnson 44 percent to 41 percent, while LBJ led McCarthy 59 to 29.[1] According to Jack Newfield, "The faces made Kennedy high. A hippie trotted alongside of his car and gave Kennedy his draft card, and Kennedy autographed it, laughing. At another point, a housewife, in a red bathrobe and her hair in curlers, ran out of her house, hugged Kennedy and got his autograph. . . . That night Kennedy, his face sunburned, and his hands scratched, said at dinner, 'I'm still not sure I can make it, but those faces, those faces all day, they seem starved. They want something. They show how much unhappiness there is in the country.'"[2]

The first speech excerpted below was given at various stops in the California campaign. In it, RFK outlines his community empowerment philosophy: "We can and will say to our cities and towns: 'Here are the funds. We expect performance. We leave the structure and management for your wisdom and talent.'" In the neoconservative era begun in 2001, this formula has been turned on its head: Unfunded mandates force the states and local communities to abide by strict federal guidelines in education, welfare, and other services and come up with the funds by either raising taxes at the state and local level or cutting other services. Governments become starved, and the services they have traditionally provided become ripe for privatization. Plum contracts go to companies and corporations that fund candidates who favor more privatization, and the government-corporate axis ends up serving only itself.

A presidential election is always a signal event in American life. When you vote, you are at one with others, often millions of others. If you choose a winner, you are glad because you think your life or life in general will change for the better. If you lose, there's always next time. But if you believe the other side stole the election, you regroup and plan and work and organize and bend every effort to win the next election. That's what the Democratic Party finally did in 2006. Howard Dean, chairman of the Democratic National Committee, adopted a fifty-state strategy to build a Democratic opposition in even the most Republican states, redeeming Robert Kennedy's 1968 vision of national reconciliation.

The second speech, given here in full, shows Kennedy honing in on his criticism of President Johnson.

Various Stops
California, March 23, 1968

This is the year when we as Americans can begin to regain control of our country. For too long we have been content to let the great issues of our time be met by bigger budgets, bigger programs, and government more and more removed from participation and control by citizens. We have assumed that more federal funds are the only answer to our problems. I believe the time has come for the leadership of America to put its trust in the hands of the people—and to meet the great domestic challenges of our time with programs shaped and run by the citizens themselves.

We can, for example, turn away from the system of welfare handouts and charity for the poor. We can begin to bring both public and private resources into our poor communities—both in urban and rural America—and give to these men and women the role of rebuilding their communities, constructing new housing, and helping to manage new industry and opportunity. This work has already begun in communities like Bedford-Stuyvesant in New York City—and I believe it can work across America.

We can and will turn away from federal programs imposed on communities. We can and will say to our cities and towns: "Here are the funds. We expect performance. We leave the structure and management for your wisdom and talent."

But this issue—the issue of the powers of the citizen—goes far beyond the problems of the poor. The loss of participation is a loss which affects all of us—whether in the suburbs of California or the towns of the Midwest and our great cities. Here, too, much can be done—and it has already begun with this campaign for new leadership in America.

For this year, those who seek new direction are participating actively in helping to change public policy. They are working in their communities, speaking to their friends, confronting their fellow-citizens, not out of special interest, not for narrow party purposes, but out of the desire to build a new America. In New Hampshire, here in California, in New York, Nebraska and Oregon, across America, the citizen of the nation is regaining control of this country's public destiny.

I believe this effort will succeed. I believe that the men and women of America will win new leadership, for themselves and their country. And out of this effort will come the spirit of discussion and debate, of confrontation and cooperation, which will begin to bridge the gaps—of age, of belief, of race, that have so divided the nation.

We shall find that our citizens have become, in the words of Jefferson, "acting members of the common government," turning their energy and their talents toward the shaping of a better America.

GREEK THEATRE, LOS ANGELES
March 24, 1968

Surrounded as we are by crisis in Vietnam, civil strife in our great cities, and a division among our people, which often erupt in dramatic forms, it is easy to overlook the most profound crisis of all: The unprecedented and perilous drift of American society away from some of its most treasured principles.

This crisis is not dramatic. It does not suddenly flare into morning headlines or across the evening television screens. The movement cannot even be noticed as we go about our daily tasks. Yet, over a period of years it has brought us to a most dangerous point. We know what this generation can accomplish.

We have had problems in the past. But at the same time we have shown that we can deal with our adversaries without bloodshed, as in the Cuban Missile Crisis. We know that we can move toward protecting mankind from nuclear disaster, as with the Test Ban Treaty. We know that this nation can be fired by idealism and will serve the needs of others by peaceful means, as through the Peace Corps. We know we can begin to reduce the tensions between black and white, and not just through laws, but personal leadership.

Together, we can make this a nation where young people do not seek the false peace of drugs. Together, we can make this a nation where old people are not shunted off; where, regardless of the color of his skin or the place of birth of his father, every citizen will have an equal chance at dignity and decency. Together, Americans are the most decent, generous, and compassionate people in the world.

Divided, they are collections of islands. Islands of blacks afraid of islands of whites. Islands of Northerners bitterly opposed to islands of Southerners. Islands of workers warring with islands of businessmen.

The sense of possibility matched to human capacity has been the central theme of our history, from the first settlers through Wilson and Roosevelt and Truman. It was the moving spirit of the Democratic Party in its proudest and most productive moments; it was the tradition of this country. Something has happened to that guiding spirit.

It is not just that policies are different or that I, and many others, disagree with what is being done. It runs far deeper than that. And much of that is that we have made a fundamental departure from the principles—not only of the Democratic Party—but of the country itself.

In specific terms the shift of deterioration is easier to see. It is most dramatically illuminated by the current disastrous course we follow in Vietnam. More than 500,000 American soldiers have been hurled into a bottomless Asian swamp against the counsel of almost every intelligent general from MacArthur to Ridgway. We know that by following the present course we cannot win a military victory—we cannot settle the war.

All that happens is ever-increasing destruction as frustration causes us to hurl more and more power against a small society. The consequences are frightening and terrible in human terms. But the very fact that our enemy is so primitive is also their greatest strength. For our power is meant to disable sophisticated, urban, technological societies. In Vietnam it is like fighting a swarm of bees with a sledge hammer. Yet all we do is to make the war larger—killing more Vietnamese and Americans—as if we could not learn the clear lessons of five years of failure.

It is obvious to almost any rational observer—not himself swept up in a position of advocacy—that we need to change these policies—and move swiftly toward a just settlement at the conference table—before our nation is further drained and its purpose corrupted by this almost unbelievable conflict.

It is, of course, not just Vietnam. Our great cities are the scene of civil strife. And yet—despite reports and warnings by group after expert group—we do not take even the basic steps needed to mount an assault on the human deprivations which are the cause of this disorder. We are doing little to improve the education of our children, restore the health and beauty of our air and water, or make our communities satisfying places in which to live. Meanwhile prices rise and so do taxes as the hard-earned prosperity of the last decades is threatened. Even the classic phrase "Sound as a dollar" has begun to seem like a rather ominous hypocrisy.

All the phrases which have meant so much to Americans—peace and progress, justice and compassion, leadership and idealism— often sound not like stirring reminders of our nation, but call forth the cynical laughter or hostility of our young and many of our adults. Not because they do not believe them, but because they do not think our leaders mean them.

These specific failures reflect the larger failure of national purpose. We do not know where we are going. We have been stripped of goals and values and direction, as we move aimlessly and rather futilely from crisis to crisis and danger to danger. And the record shows that kind of approach will not only not solve problems, it will only deepen them.

This is not simply the result of bad policies and lack of skill. It flows from the fact that for almost the first time the national leadership is calling upon the darker impulses of the American spirit—not, perhaps, deliberately, but through its action and the example it sets—an example where integrity, truth, honor, and all the rest seem like words to fill out speeches rather than guiding beliefs. Thus we are turned inward. People wish to protect what they have. There is a failing of generosity and compassion. There is an unwillingness to sacrifice or take risks. All of this is contrary to the deepest and most dominant impulses of the American character—all that which has characterized two centuries of history.

The issue in this election, therefore, is whether this new and startling path shall continue into the future, or whether we shall turn back to our roots and to our tradition, so that future historians shall view this period as the great aberration of American history. That is the issue you must decide this year. That is why I am running. Not simply to become President of the United States. Not simply because I have new ideas and new programs and new policies. But because I hope to offer you in the form of my candidacy—because that is the only way our system allows such a choice—I hope to offer you a way in which the people themselves can lead the way back to those ideals which are the source of national strength and generosity and compassion of deed.

7

The Grand Alliance

VISITING FRANCE IN December 1966, RFK had noted consistent opposition to the American war in Vietnam. The French had fought a war there before, beginning in 1946, and been defeated at their last stand, at Dien Bien Phu, eight years later. President Charles de Gaulle and the Socialist leader François Mitterrand, who would himself become president in 1981, both warned Kennedy against the war. The novelist and culture minister André Malraux told him, "The United States cannot do well when you are involved in a matter of inner contradiction. Vietnam is against American tradition."[1] The grand alliance built up after World War II between the Europeans and Americans was rent by the Vietnam war, fought more or less unilaterally by Johnson, with some token help from the Australians. America's most important allies, such as France and the United Kingdom, opposed the war.

SALINAS/MONTEREY
California, March 24, 1968

This is a time to create, not destroy. This is a time for men to work out of a sense of decency, not bitterness. This is a time to begin again. . . . As we stand here today, brave young men are fighting across an ocean. Here, while the moon shines, men are dying on the other side of the earth. Which of them might have written a great poem? Which of them would have cured cancer? Which of them might have played in a World Series or given us the gift of laughter from a stage or helped build a bridge or a university? Which of them might have taught a child to read? It is our responsibility to let those men live. . . .

There are other tasks before us. It is a time to begin rebuilding the Grand Alliance—to repair the bonds of trust and confidence of those historic allies whose friendship has been the basis of our own security so many times in the past. It is a time to recall ourselves to our true responsibilities in the world: to recognize that we cannot sit frozen in indifference while every day, 10,000 fellow human beings starve elsewhere in the world; that it is a monstrous disproportion that we should buy eight million new cars a year while most of the world goes without shoes.

There is difficulty and division in the land. But in the last six days, I have been to Kansas and Alabama, Tennessee and my own state of New York: and now I have come to California. And I think I see the stirrings of something new. It is not the creation of any candidate or leader. It is nothing I made. It is a sense of possibility, that the American people are discovering for themselves.

Some of them are young in years. All of them are young in spirit.

They are beginning to feel that change is possible—that hope is possible—that by the work of their own hands, and the love of their own hearts, they can restore that fundamental sense of decency for themselves, for each other, and for their posterity. There is a small minority that seems to believe that the way to further their cause is to shout down government officials. But the alienated and the apathetic alike, I believe, will dwindle in number and decline in strength—and finally they too will see, as more and more are seeing every day, that we can make a difference. We can put our beloved country together again. We can turn our course around.

8

"... through the eyes of the poor"

RFK FELT A profound kinship with the dispossessed. According to Arthur Schlesinger, Jr., at a meeting of Oklahomans for Indian Opportunity in 1967, "Answering one question, he said, at once jokingly and seriously, 'I wish I had been born an Indian.'" Oklahoma Senator Fred Harris, whose wife was Native American, said, "It sounded so real and also kind of wistfully funny that everybody laughed and applauded." As President Kennedy's closest adviser, RFK often had to play "bad cop" to JFK's "good cop" and got a reputation for being ruthless. Vine Deloria, Jr., who wrote *Custer Died for Your Sins*, said that Native Americans thought Kennedy "as great a hero as the most famous Indian war chiefs precisely because of his ruthlessness." They "saw him as a warrior, the white Crazy Horse. . . . Spiritually, he was an Indian."[1]

Kennedy was also a champion of the rights of one of the most ignored and abused groups of society, migrant farm workers, and over the years had become a friend of César Chávez, the head of the National Farm Workers Association, later the United Farm

Workers of America. Chávez was two years younger than RFK, and his heroes were Saint Francis and Gandhi. "For all their differences in background," writes Arthur Schlesinger, Jr., "the two men were rather alike: both short, shy, familial, devout, opponents of violence, with strong veins of melancholy and fatalism." Kennedy wrote in a 1967 article entitled "Crisis in Our Cities," "If we try to look through the eyes of the young slum-dweller—the Negro, the Puerto Rican, and the Mexican-American—the world is a dark and hopeless place." Chávez said, "He could see things through the eyes of the poor. . . . It was like he was ours."[2]

It was a visit to Chávez on March 10, 1968, that finally tipped the balance for RFK to run for the presidency. Chávez was ending a twenty-five-day hunger strike to protest working conditions in the fields. There is a famous photograph of the two men breaking the fast during a communion. Chávez had lost thirty-five pounds and was weak from the fast but noticed that Kennedy's hands were bleeding from his own constant communion with the crowds. "Kennedy praised Chávez as a hero of our times then said to the crowd, 'Let me say to you that violence is no answer.'"[3]

OLVERA STREET
Los Angeles, California, March 24, 1968

Two weeks ago, I came to California to pay homage to one of the great living Americans: César Chávez. For more than two years from his base in the grape fields of California, César Chávez has been sending the rest of America a message.

The message says that Americans of Mexican descent were walking taller than ever before. The message says that dignity is not something awarded coldly in a welfare office. The message says that dignity is something a man attains with his mind, with the labor of his body, with his belief in himself. It is not something you buy in a supermarket.

I come here to honor César Chávez, and to honor his message. I come here today for other reasons. But my concerns remain the same concerns of César Chávez.

I come here because America is a divided nation. I come here because America has become a nation which will spend $36 billion this year on the far side of the earth in Vietnam, and somehow cannot raise money for a school lunch program. I come here because there are too many people in our country who no longer feel the government cares for them.

I come here because I believe that it is the business of government to allow free men to live in dignity. How can a man retain his dignity when a welfare system shames him? I believe that men would rather work at disagreeable jobs than accept the humiliation of a handout. . . .

This week an American of Mexican descent, Raul Rojas, fights for the featherweight championship of the world. I wish him my best but this country must insure that Mexican Americans do not have to bleed for a living.

I want to see an America where Mexican Americans produce featherweight champions of the world, but also space engineers, doctors of letters, great novelists, fine composers and Nobel Prize winners.

Here before us today there are hundreds of young people. America should allow them to be anything which their talent and intelligence can make them. If America fails these young people, if through indifference or callousness they are denied jobs, opportunities, or education, then the American dream will have failed.

I do not believe that America will fail. Together we can build an America that can give these children the open door to the future. That is why I am here.

I am here to run for the President of the United States and I need your help. I need your help because I believe all Americans can work together. Together, we can destroy the slums, together we can harness rivers and preserve forests. Together we can make ourselves a nation that spends more on books than on bombs, more on hospitals than the terrible tools of war, more on decent houses than military aircraft.

Together we can do all of this. United we are a nation. Divided we are nothing. I think we can build a new America. We can start building that new America now. I want to see an America that guarantees dignity now. I want to see an America that guarantees that freedom, equality, and hope are not empty abstractions, but realities. No. I want to see an America where a young man who is asked to bleed in Vietnam for the freedom of strangers is guaranteed freedom of equality and hope in his own country.

Together we can make a beginning and tomorrow our children can go forth together to explore the stars. That is why I am here. That is why I am asking for our help. That is why I run for President of the United States.

9

The Spirit of the Young

IN 1968, EVERY young man in the United States was subject to being drafted into the army and sent to Vietnam, unless he had a severe physical infirmity, which disqualified him, or a less severe one, which made him eligible for noncombatant service only. College and university students in good standing could receive draft deferments. Those who opposed war in general on religious grounds could become conscientious objectors and were obliged to perform alternative service. Every other young man—and these were disproportionately poor or working-class—had to serve, most likely in Vietnam. Speaking at Idaho State University in late March to an audience many of whom had received student deferments, RFK noted the unfairness of the situation: "We must realize that the system from which we have sent a disproportionate number of Negroes, Mexican-Americans to fight in Vietnam is a faulty one." He then said he advocated abolition of deferments from the draft.[1] It was part of his political persona; he "positively delighted in baiting voters he found too smug."[2]

There was a slogan in the 1960s, "Don't trust anyone over thirty." It was mostly about the Vietnam war, I think. White men over forty had gotten us into it, and the war had come to dominate the lives of men under thirty, so I understood the reason. I was twenty-five in 1968, and against the war, but I thought that was a pretty silly slogan. I trusted a lot of people over thirty. How could we live into the future if we didn't trust at least some of the over-thirties, especially the antiwar activists Dr. Benjamin Spock (sixty-five in 1968), Jean-Paul Sartre (sixty-three), and Bertrand Russell (ninety-six!)?

But "Don't trust anyone over thirty" also meant that sometimes, and 1968 was one of those times, it was good to look at things with fresh eyes, to put the past behind you, and to see with the eyes of the young.

It is the dream of every politician to tap into the usually unfocused, usually noncommunal energies of young people. In 1968 it was there in the campaigns of both Eugene McCarthy (which was even called the Children's Crusade) and RFK. As he was deciding whether to run, RFK told a friend that he had "a lot of enemies—business, labor, the newspapers, even most of the politicians." Who was for him, she asked? "The young, the minorities, the Negroes and the Puerto Ricans," he replied.[3]

An army of young volunteers is the nightmare of every politician who does not appeal to the young, however. Richard Nixon's worst nightmare was to run against another Kennedy, aided by armies of the young, and be defeated again, as he had been in 1960.

In this speech, RFK calls for a national effort to broaden the base of the Democratic Party: "to organize ourselves, and carry our message to hundreds of thousands of others, and then go to the meetings, work in the precinct caucuses and district and state conventions; we have to become, in Jefferson's phrase, acting members of the common government."

WEBER STATE COLLEGE
Ogden, Utah, March 27, 1968

We are often told that the young people of today are in rebellion.

In recent days, we have seen how true this image can be. Young people are striking at the core of authority. Students at universities are demanding the rights of free speech and assembly. They are demanding a voice in their own education. Meanwhile, the government urges order. It appeals to their patriotism. It points to the danger of foreign enemies. It threatens them with expulsion, imprisonment, and conscription into the army.

But these students are not at Berkeley, or Michigan, or Harvard. They are in Warsaw, and Cracow, and Prague—and in Moscow, too. What these students are fighting for—and what they appear to have won in Czechoslovakia—is not a victory of ideology, but a victory of spirit. It is the same spirit which has been heard in the courtrooms of Moscow, in the streets of Spain, and on the campuses of the United States: and that is the spirit of youth.

The youthfulness I speak of is not a time of life, but a state of mind, a temper of the will, a quality of the imagination, a predominance of courage over timidity, of the appetite for adventure over the love of ease. It is the spirit which knows the difference between force and reason. It does not accept the failures of today as a reason for the cruelties of tomorrow. It believes that one man can make a difference—and that men of good will, working together, can grasp the future and mold it to our will.

This is the spirit I want to see return to the United States—and that is why I run for President.

For this is the spirit that gave this nation the strength to be formed. It has sustained us at every crisis. And it has impressed itself on men all over the world. It has inspired the writers of Russia to defy the might of a garrison state, citing the words and principles of our Constitution and our Bill of Rights. It has even impressed Ho Chi Minh, who began his war against the French by quoting not Marx or Mao, but our Declaration of Independence.

How ironic it is then, that at a time when our own example spreads the seeds of liberty abroad and at home, there are some who see danger in the exercise of that liberty here in America, where it all began. They decry the growth of dissent: they urge that "the time has come to unite . . . to support our leaders, our government." And they ask us, "Whose side are you on?"

I think the time has come to answer that question.

I am on the side of those who seek a new effort for an end to the war in Vietnam—a war that has cost us 20,000 lives, 50 billions of dollars, and a decade of struggle; all to bring us no closer to the victory we always proclaimed was just around the corner.

I am on the side of those who seek an end to this war, not by unilateral American withdrawal—nor by further fruitless escalation—

but by an active effort to win a negotiated settlement in Vietnam, by diminishing the bloodshed, expanding the base of the Saigon government, and recognizing that our principal adversary—the National Liberation Front—will play a role in the political future of South Vietnam. And as one who was involved in many of the past decisions concerning Vietnam, I am on the side of those who are not afraid to admit past mistakes. . . .

If we want to change the course the nation is on, we cannot wait until November—not unless we want to wait for Richard Nixon. We have to work now, to win the Democratic nomination in August.

And to do that, we . . . have to enormously broaden the base of the Democratic Party: to organize ourselves, and carry our message to hundreds of thousands of others, and then go to the meetings, work in the precinct caucuses and district and state conventions; we have to become, in Jefferson's phrase, acting members of the common government. When we do this, we will win the nomination—and we will win the election.

But having done it, we will have done much more. We will have opened up an opportunity for a substantial change in the structure of government in this country. And that is also necessary. To return to the local community real power to act on the conditions which shape men's lives—the education of their children, the design and renewal of their cities, the recreational facilities of their rural areas—to bring back that kind of control has been a dream of liberals and conservatives alike for many years. What we have lacked, however, has been organized and sustained political demand from local institutions capable of managing the programs. But now I think we will have them.

For I believe that once the active and concerned citizens of this nation organize, and build new bonds between themselves, to reassert control over our political lives—once we have done that, we will also be able to assert control over the government programs which so deeply affect our personal lives.

And a federal government which really wants to return that control to local communities—to counties in rural areas, down to neighborhoods within large cities—will have an actively involved citizenry ready and able to assume that control. . . .

≡ 10 ≡

Johnson Withdraws

THROUGHOUT 1967 and into 1968, Lyndon Johnson kept saying that things would get better in Vietnam, but they never did. Now he was suffering from what was becoming known as the credibility gap. He had won the 1964 presidential election in a landslide, but in a Gallup poll taken in late March 1968 only 26 percent of the nation approved of how Johnson was conducting the war, while 36 percent approved of his overall job performance.[1]

He later told the historian Doris Kearns Goodwin about this period: "The thing I feared most from the first day of my presidency was actually coming true. Robert Kennedy had openly announced his intention to reclaim the throne in the memory of his brother. And the American people, swayed by the magic of the name, were dancing in the streets."[2]

On the night of March 31, 1968, President Johnson was scheduled to give a nationally televised address. It was assumed that he would announce a new peace initiative to influence the Wisconsin primary two days later in his favor. And in the first part of his speech, he did declare a reduction in the bombing of North Vietnam. As Jack Newfield writes, "Johnson's mania for secrecy prevailed. . . . His statement of withdrawal from the race was not included in the text of his remarks distributed in advance." He ended his speech with the bombshell:

"With American sons in the fields far away, with America's future under challenge right here at home, with our hopes and the world's hopes for peace in the balance every day, I do not believe that I should devote an hour, or a day, of my time to any personal partisan causes. Or to any duties other than the awesome duties of this office—the Presidency of your country.

"Accordingly I shall not seek, and I will not accept, the nomination of my party for another term as your President."[3]

STATEMENT ON JOHNSON'S DECISION NOT TO SEEK REELECTION
Overseas Press Club
New York, New York, April 1, 1968

Last night I sent the President the following telegram:

"Mr. President:

First of all, let me say that I fervently hope that your new efforts for peace in Vietnam will succeed. Your decision regarding the presidency subordinates self to country and is truly magnanimous. I respectfully and earnestly request an opportunity to visit with you as soon as possible to discuss how we might work together in the interest of national unity during the coming months. Sincerely, Robert F. Kennedy."

That wire sums up much of what I want to say today. The President's action reflects both courage and generosity of spirit. In these past sixteen days, I have been in some eighteen states, North, South, East, and West. In Alabama and in Watts, in New York and in New Mexico, in Washington, D.C. and in Washington State, wherever I went, I found Americans of all ages and colors and political beliefs deeply desirous of peace in Vietnam and reconciliation here at home. Despite all the discord and dispirit, despite all the extremists and their actions, there remains, in this country today, an enormous reservoir of hope and goodwill. Americans want to move forward; they want to better their communities, to make this country not only more livable for all Americans but a shining example for all the world.

To free their energies for progress at home, they want peace in Vietnam—produced not by the surrender of either side, but by a negotiated settlement that realistically takes into account, as quickly as possible, the need for all Vietnamese, and only Vietnamese, to determine the future course of that country. I have long urged that we make the first move in this direction by de-escalating our military effort, halting our bombing of the North, insisting upon reforms in the South, and pressing for negotiations with all parties looking toward a transfer of the present conflict from the military to the political arena. I am hopeful that the actions announced by the President will prove to be a step in the journey toward peace. It is obviously a critical time, and I think it would be inappropriate to offer any detached comments regarding those actions at this time.

As we move toward a political resolution of the agony of Vietnam, we can start to redirect our national resources and energies toward the vital problems of our national community. The crisis of our cities, the tension among our races, the complexities of a society at once so rich and so deprived: all of these call urgently for our best efforts. We must reach across the false barriers that divide us from our brothers and countrymen, to seek and find peace abroad, reconciliation at home, and the participation in the life of our country that is the deepest desire of the American people and the truest expression of our national goals. In this spirit I will continue my campaign for the Presidency.

≡ 11 ≡

Community Development

Peter Edelman, an aide to Robert Kennedy, notes that RFK bristled at being called a liberal[1]—but more, he bristled at being labeled, period. In fact, for five months in the early 1950s, when RFK served as an aide to red-baiting Senator Joseph McCarthy, he had been anathema to liberals, and many liberals still distrusted and even hated him. But people grow and change, and few more than RFK. Eleanor Roosevelt, the widow of FDR and the keeper of the flame of liberalism, resisted him almost until her death in November 1962, but her son, Franklin D. Roosevelt, Jr., said that RFK became "the torch-bearer of everything that my mother stood for and fought for."[2]

Liberalism comprised the great programs of FDR's administration, such as Social Security, as well as unemployment compensation and Medicare. Johnson's congressional agenda, his War on Poverty in particular, was classic old-style liberalism, and RFK felt it relied far too much on government bureaucracy. Some way surely could be found to help the poor work their own way out of poverty.

But how? An idea, germinated in early 1966, was to bring business into the poorest neighborhoods. On February 4, 1966, RFK toured the rundown Brooklyn area called Bedford-Stuyvesant, which had 400,000 residents—80 percent black, 15 percent Puerto Rican, 5 percent white. A woman yelled at him, "You politicians come out here and nothing changes." He asked a local official what the community needed. "A swimming pool for the kids," came the reply. Later, back in Manhattan, Kennedy said, "Work it out. Get them a swimming pool." Then a little later: "We gotta do better than a swimming pool." He asked his aides to find a way to help Bed-Stuy rebuild.[3]

They came up with a plan for a community corporation with two boards—"one for the black community leaders to propose ideas for redevelopment, and another for Kennedy's white business friends to provide professionalism and resources." A grant of $750,000 was approved by McGeorge Bundy, head of the Ford Foundation. (Bundy, who had been in the Kennedy and Johnson administrations, was one of the best and brightest who had brought us the Vietnam war and was doing penance by working for good at the Ford Foundation.) On December 10, 1966, the Bedford-Stuyvesant Restoration Corporation was launched. At the opening press conference, "Kennedy presided proudly over captains of industry and civic-minded black housewives." As Evan Thomas describes it, "The Bedford-Stuyvesant Corporation was his kind of organization: small, anti-bureaucratic, seemingly democratic but in fact tightly controlled, operating outside the mainstream and proud of it."[4]

HOTEL GRANADA, ASHLAND PLACE
Bedford-Stuyvesant, New York, April 1, 1968

We meet here today to celebrate a triumph of cooperation and mutual understanding—to celebrate the fact that a new joint venture between the residents of Bedford-Stuyvesant and the business community is under way.

We meet to salute the achievement of the Bedford-Stuyvesant community corporations—the Restoration Corporation that is ably led by Judge Jones and Frank Thomas, and the Development and Services Corporation, headed by Douglas Dillon and John Doar. We meet to salute the contribution of more than 80 banks and insurance companies, and leadership of Mr. George Moore, who have lent their skill and understanding—and their money—to this venture. And most of all, we salute the people of Bedford-Stuyvesant, for their faith in one another and their devotion to a common cause.

Since last fall, these groups have been working together towards the goal which has now been reached—the creation of a healthy mortgage market for Bedford-Stuyvesant—a giant step forward on the road to a healthy and prosperous economy for this community.

As a result of these efforts, twenty applications for FHA-guaranteed mortgages are now in the hands of the Restoration Corporation—applications which, when approved, will enable people to reduce their mortgage payments by as much as 33 per cent—to rehabilitate their homes, to buy and sell homes with the same ease that people in other neighborhoods take for granted.

The story of this venture is a perfect example of how these corporations can bring about meaningful social change in Bedford-Stuyvesant.

First, residents of the community—working through the Restoration Corporation—identified the need for long-term mortgage money as a major priority for the community. For years, they had been forced to make substantial down payments in order to get any kind of mortgage. Then they had to obtain not one mortgage but two or even three. And these mortgages were always short-term—they had to be paid over only five or ten years.

This situation has drastic consequences for the community; monthly payments were so high that most people couldn't afford to spend any money to improve their homes. Even if they had the money to spend, there was no incentive to improve their homes, because the investment was frozen into the property by the lack of willing or able purchasers; and in many cases, people were forced to take in boarders.

The lack of mortgage money thus deserved a major part of the responsibility for the deterioration of much of the housing in the community. It was responsible for the fact that there are now over 300 abandoned buildings in Bedford-Stuyvesant—buildings which could not be rehabilitated because the money wasn't there.

The people agreed that the cooperation of commercial leaders was essential if this cycle was to be broken. So they went to the Development and Services Corporation, where they found a ready understanding of the problem. The result was a commitment by more than 80 banks and insurance companies to stake 25-year mortgages solely on the basis of FHA approval. The Restoration Corporation will review applications, send them to the FHA—and once the FHA gives the green light, each of the financial institutions in turn will lend the money.

This money will enable the citizens of Bedford-Stuyvesant to keep their homes in good repair. It will enable them to remain in the community, contributing to its growth and strength. It will bring jobs to the skilled workers of the community—so that the experience gained last summer in the important job of rehabilitating the homes of Bedford-Stuyvesant will be put to work for their benefit and the benefit of the community. It will enable people to buy and improve the abandoned buildings that now scar the face of Bedford-Stuyvesant, and that until now could not economically be rehabilitated.

This program is not the whole answer to the housing needs of Bedford-Stuyvesant. Only one-to-four-family dwellings are covered by it. So the challenging problem of improving the neighborhood's multiple dwellings will remain. The task of attracting industrial investment still lies ahead. And much more remains to be done before the residents of Bedford-Stuyvesant will have the healthy, prosperous community they want and deserve.

But the program that the corporations have announced today marks another step towards that goal, which only a few years ago seemed beyond hope. It demonstrates the power of an organized community to take direction of its destiny. It demonstrates the power of a close collaboration between cities and the business community to give people a concrete opportunity to turn around the decline of their neighborhood.

So today we celebrate both an achievement and a symbol—we take pride in the fact that hundreds, perhaps thousands of homes will be rehabilitated—and that a community organization has proved that it can plan its future and make that plan work. Where others have announced grand schemes for the future, Bedford-Stuyvesant has accomplished one vital task here and now.

We live in a time when the nation is deeply divided. But you have proven that we need not remain so. Together we can attack the problems that seem so overwhelming, and master them. Your example should give courage to all Americans in the difficult days before us.

12

On the Death of Martin Luther King, Jr.

MARTIN LUTHER KING, JR., did more for the cause of civil rights for all people than any other American in our history. Because of his work and his absolute devotion to nonviolent means, in the tradition of Gandhi, he was awarded the Nobel Peace Prize in 1964. On April 4, 1967, exactly one year before his death, he committed himself to opposition to the Vietnam war in a speech at New York City's Riverside Church. He said something that evening that many Americans, and much of the world, feel because of the invasion and occupation of Iraq: "The greatest purveyor of violence in the world today is my own government."[1]

A year later, he was in Memphis to support a sanitation workers' strike. There had been threats against his life there as almost everywhere he went. He was planning a massive event, a poor people's march on Washington, for April 22.

Like most of the world, I was astounded that, his last night on earth, Martin Luther King seemed to predict his own death.

"Well, I don't know what will happen now; we've got some difficult days ahead. But it really doesn't matter with me now, because I've been to the mountaintop. And I don't mind. Like anybody, I would like to live a long life—longevity has its place. But I'm not concerned about that now. I just want to do God's will. And He's allowed me to go up to the mountain. And I've looked over, and I've seen the Promised Land. I may not get there with you. But I want you to know tonight, that we, as a people, will get to the Promised Land. And so I'm happy tonight; I'm not worried about anything; I'm not fearing any man. Mine eyes have seen the glory of the coming of the Lord."

The next day he was shot dead. He was thirty-nine.

When RFK landed in Indianapolis, the city's police chief urged him to cancel his appearance at a political rally in a black neighborhood. Who knew what kind of reaction would occur? A white man would be breaking the news to a black audience that a black leader had been assassinated by a white man. But Kennedy went ahead, and the extemporaneous speech that follows shows his bravery, his moral sense, and his understanding of tragedy.

That night, there were riots in 110 cities, but none in Indianapolis, where RFK had spoken.[2]

INDIANAPOLIS, INDIANA
April 4, 1968

Ladies and gentlemen. I'm only going to talk to you for a minute or so this evening because I have some very sad news for all of you.

I have bad news for you, for all of our fellow citizens, and people who love peace all over the world, and that is that Martin Luther King was shot and killed tonight.

Martin Luther King dedicated his life to love and to justice for his fellow human beings, and he died because of that effort.

In this difficult day, in this difficult time for the United States, it is perhaps well to ask what kind of a nation we are and what direction we want to move in. For those of you who are black—considering the evidence there evidently is that there were white people who were responsible—you can be filled with bitterness, with hatred, and a desire for revenge. We can move in that direction as a country, in great polarization—black people amongst black, white people amongst white, filled with hatred toward one another.

Or we can make an effort, as Martin Luther King did, to understand and to comprehend, and to replace that violence, that stain of bloodshed that has spread across our land, with an effort to understand with compassion and love.

For those of you who are black and are tempted to be filled with hatred and distrust at the injustice of such an act, against all white people, I can only say that I feel in my own heart the same kind of feeling. I had a member of my family killed, but he was killed by a white man. But we have to make an effort in the United States, we have to make an effort to understand, to go beyond these rather difficult times.

My favorite poet was Aeschylus. He wrote: "In our sleep, pain which cannot forget falls drop by drop upon the heart until, in our own despair, against our will, comes wisdom through the awful grace of God."

What we need in the United States is not division; what we need in the United States is not hatred; what we need in the United States is not violence or lawlessness; but love and wisdom, and compassion toward one another, and a feeling of justice toward those who still suffer within our country, whether they be white or they be black.

So I shall ask you tonight to return home, to say a prayer for the family of Martin Luther King, that's true, but more importantly to say a prayer for our own country, which all of us love—a prayer for understanding and that compassion of which I spoke.

We can do well in this country. We will have difficult times; we've had difficult times in the past; we will have difficult times in the future. It is not the end of violence; it is not the end of lawlessness; it is not the end of disorder.

But the vast majority of white people and the vast majority of black people in this country want to live together, want to improve the quality of our life, and want justice for all human beings who abide in our land.

Let us dedicate ourselves to what the Greeks wrote so many years ago: to tame the savageness of man and make gentle the life of this world.

Let us dedicate ourselves to that, and say a prayer for our country and for our people.

☰ 13 ☰

On the Mindless Menace of Violence

THE NIGHT OF April 4, RFK called Martin Luther King, Jr.'s widow, Coretta Scott King, to express his condolences and offer to put a plane at her disposal to take her husband's body from Memphis to Atlanta. She accepted. Later, remembering JFK and RFK, she said: "Although they were political figures, they were human beings first, and their humanness reached out to the needs of people." The riots after King's assassination left thirty-nine people dead, most of them black; 75,000 National Guard and federal troops were called up.[1]

Kennedy canceled his regular schedule, and on April 5 spoke briefly in Cleveland.

CITY CLUB OF CLEVELAND
April 5, 1968

This is a time of shame and sorrow. It is not a day for politics. I have saved this one opportunity, my only event of today, to speak briefly to you about the mindless menace of violence in America which again stains our land and every one of our lives.

It is not the concern of any one race. The victims of the violence are black and white, rich and poor, young and old, famous and unknown. They are, most important of all, human beings whom other human beings loved and needed. No one—no matter where he lives or what he does—can be certain who will suffer from some senseless act of bloodshed. And yet it goes on and on and on in this country of ours.

Why? What has violence ever accomplished? What has it ever created? No martyr's cause has ever been stilled by an assassin's bullet.

No wrongs have ever been righted by riots and civil disorders. A sniper is only a coward, not a hero; and an uncontrolled, uncontrollable mob is only the voice of madness, not the voice of reason.

Whenever any American's life is taken by another American unnecessarily—whether it is done in the name of the law or in the defiance of the law, by one man or a gang, in cold blood or in passion, in an attack of violence or in response to violence—whenever we tear at the fabric of the life which another man has painfully and clumsily woven for himself and his children, the whole nation is degraded.

"Among free men," said Abraham Lincoln, "there can be no successful appeal from the ballot to the bullet; and those who take such appeal are sure to lose their cause and pay the costs."

Yet we seemingly tolerate a rising level of violence that ignores our common humanity and our claims to civilization alike. We calmly accept newspaper reports of civilian slaughter in far-off lands. We glorify killing on movie and television screens and call it entertainment. We make it easy for men of all shades of sanity to acquire whatever weapons and ammunition they desire.

Too often we honor swagger and bluster and wielders of force; too often we excuse those who are willing to build their own lives on the shattered dreams of others. Some Americans who preach non-violence abroad fail to practice it here at home. Some who accuse others of inciting riots have by their own conduct invited them.

Some look for scapegoats, others look for conspiracies, but this much is clear: violence breeds violence, repression brings retaliation, and only a cleansing of our whole society can remove this sickness from our soul.

For there is another kind of violence, slower but just as deadly destructive as the shot or the bomb in the night. This is the violence of institutions; indifference and inaction and slow decay. This is the violence that afflicts the poor, that poisons relations between men because their skin has different colors. This is the slow destruction of a child by hunger, and schools without books and homes without heat in the winter.

This is the breaking of a man's spirit by denying him the chance to stand as a father and as a man among other men. And this too afflicts us all.

I have not come here to propose a set of specific remedies nor is there a single set. For a broad and adequate outline we know what must be done. When you teach a man to hate and fear his brother, when you teach that he is a lesser man because of his color or his beliefs or the policies he pursues, when you teach that those who differ from you threaten your freedom or your job or your family, then you also learn to confront others not as fellow citizens but as enemies, to be met not with cooperation but with conquest; to be subjugated and mastered.

We learn, at the last, to look at our brothers as aliens, men with whom we share a city, but not a community; men bound to us in common dwelling, but not in common effort. We learn to share only a common fear, only a common desire to retreat from each other, only a common impulse to meet disagreement with force. For all this, there are no final answers.

Yet we know what we must do. It is to achieve true justice among our fellow citizens. The question is not what programs we should seek to enact. The question is whether we can find in our own midst and in our own hearts that leadership of humane purpose that will recognize the terrible truths of our existence.

We must admit the vanity of our false distinctions among men and learn to find our own advancement in the search for the advancement of others. We must admit in ourselves that our own children's future cannot be built on the misfortunes of others. We must recognize that this short life can neither be ennobled or enriched by hatred or revenge.

Our lives on this planet are too short and the work to be done too great to let this spirit flourish any longer in our land. Of course we cannot vanquish it with a program, nor with a resolution.

But we can perhaps remember, if only for a time, that those who live with us are our brothers, that they share with us the same short moment of life; that they seek, as do we, nothing but the chance to live out their lives in purpose and in happiness, winning what satisfaction and fulfillment they can.

Surely, this bond of common faith, this bond of common goal, can begin to teach us something. Surely, we can learn, at least, to look at those around us as fellow men, and surely we can begin to work a little harder to bind up the wounds among us and to become in our own hearts brothers and countrymen once again.

≡ 14 ≡

In Black America

RFK ATTENDED KING'S funeral in Atlanta on April 7, along with McCarthy, Humphrey, and two contenders for the Republican nomination, Richard Nixon and Nelson Rockefeller. But the president didn't attend, and Kennedy "observed, without bravado, that lack of physical courage" had kept Johnson away.[1]

After the funeral, RFK met with some of King's closest associates—Ralph Abernathy, Hosea Williams, James Bevel, and Andrew Young (who would become the first black mayor of Atlanta and after that President Jimmy Carter's ambassador to the United Nations). There was anger and grief and a good deal of venting, and someone asked whether Kennedy actually had a program for racial justice. RFK replied that he had "some ideas. . . . But really I didn't come here to discuss politics. That would be in the worst taste. I just came to pay tribute to a man I had a lot of respect for." Young recalled, "It was very embarrassing because you got the impression . . . well, that in a way, he was more sensitive to the situation than some of us were." Because of this meeting,

Young came to believe that "white America does have someone in it who cares."[2] In the next two speeches excerpted here, RFK outlines some of his ideas for achieving racial justice.

SCOTTISH RITE BANQUET HALL
Fort Wayne, Indiana, April 10, 1968

The death of Dr. Martin Luther King is one of those huge events that signals a turning point in our nation's history. Although it is charged with immediate tragedy and personal grief, it also flows from the three centuries in which black men have lived on this continent. Like many shattering moments, it is like a gap in time itself, whose meaning is obscure and whose consequences are neither known nor inevitable. It could be the beginning of a final successful effort to make one nation of all our people—equal in justice and in opportunity. Or it could foretell a continuing civil strife which threatens to transform our cities into armed camps and our streets into passageways for violence and fear. . . .

Seeing around them the abundance of America, and hearing the promises of leaders, [Negroes] have been awakened to hope. A changing world has made them aware and proud of their full worth and dignity as human beings. And many Negroes— especially among the young—are losing faith in the good-will and purpose of the nation and its institutions. Frustrated hope and loss of faith breed desperation. And desperate men take to the streets. . . .

There is no sure way to suppress men filled with anger who feel they have nothing to lose. That is an important lesson of the modern age. In the past several nights there has been a curfew in Washington. Any person—white or black—who has ventured out into the streets after dark has been stopped and questioned by troops and police. Only those who can justify their journey are allowed to proceed. And no person has traveled through the city by day or night without at least some apprehension of violence.

This is a necessary precaution, but in the long run we cannot live this way; not if we wish to keep the country we know. Should we be forced to turn our cities into garrisons then the liberty of every citizen will be diminished. If we do not bring about lasting peace then the day may come when no one will be able to send his child to school or to take a bus without fear. We must act, therefore, not only for the sake of the Negro, but for all of us and for the nation.

It is too easy to say that other minorities found their own way, even if that were completely true. For we must remember that the progress of many groups, including my own ancestors, the Irish, was not unmarked by violence, repression, and hatred. But none of these groups had a heritage which helped destroy tradition and culture and in which it was dangerous for a black man to presume to learning. Gradually and painfully Negroes themselves are overcoming this legacy, but it is not easy. Other minorities got their start by going West or working as laborers, so their sons could study to become mechanics, and their sons could become lawyers or even politicians. Today we live in a vast and complicated world of sprawling cities and huge industries, all of it moved by intricate technology and elaborate organization. It takes help for a poor man in a black ghetto to find a place in such a world. In fact, it is hard for all the rest of us. And, too, this is the only American minority with a black skin. I doubt there are many of us who, if they look honestly into their own hearts, will not admit that this makes a difference.

So there is our problem. Among us are millions who wish to be part of this society—to share its abundance, its opportunity, and its purposes. We can deny this wish or work to make it come true. If we choose denial then we choose spreading conflict, which will surely erode the well-being and liberty of every citizen and, in a profound way, diminish the idea of America. If we choose fulfillment it will take work but we will choose to improve the well-being of all our people; choose to end fear and heal wounds; and we will choose peace—the only peace that can last—peace with justice. . . .

MICHIGAN STATE UNIVERSITY
East Lansing, Michigan, April 11, 1968

. . . Through the eyes of the white majority, the Negro world is one of steady and continuous progress. In a few years, he has seen the entire structure of discriminatory legislation torn down. He has heard Presidents become spokesmen for racial justice, while black Americans enter the cabinet and the Supreme Court. The white American has paid taxes for poverty and education programs, and watched his children risk their lives to register voters in Alabama.

Seeing this, he asks, what cause can there be for violent insurrection, of dissatisfaction with present progress? But if we try to look through the eyes of the young slum-dweller—the Negro, and the Puerto Rican, and the Mexican American—the world is a dark and hopeless place indeed. Let us look for a moment. The chances are that he was born into a family without a father, often as a result of welfare laws which require a broken home as a condition for help. I have seen, in my own state of New York, these children crowded with adults into one or two rooms, without adequate plumbing or heat, each night trying to defend against marauding rats. The growing child goes to a school which teaches little that helps him in an alien world. The chances are seven of ten that he will not graduate from high school; and even when he does, he has a fifty-fifty chance of acquiring only as much as the equivalent of an eighth grade education. A young college graduate who taught in a ghetto school sums it up this way: "The books are junk, the paint peels, the cellar stinks, the teachers call you nigger, the windows fall in on your head."

For the rest of life also there are statistics: 43 percent of ghetto housing substandard and overcrowded; 14,000 people treated for rat bites every year; a quarter of a million Puerto Rican school children in New York City, of whom only 37 percent went to college last year. Most important, the people of the ghetto live today with an unemployment rate far worse than the rest of the nation knew during the depth of the Great Depression.

That was a national emergency. Our cities therefore envelop dozens of even greater emergencies. In the typical big-city ghetto, only two out of five men have jobs which pay $60 per week or more—enough for each member of a family of four to eat 70 cents worth of food a day. Only half the adult men have full-time jobs at any rate of pay.

Barely three out of five have any work at all. And let us be clear that all this is true despite the laws, despite the programs, despite all the speeches and promises of the last seven years. It must be for us a cruel and humbling fact—but it is a fact nonetheless— that our efforts have not even maintained the problem as it was: economic and social conditions in these areas, says the Department of Labor, are growing worse, not better.

But this is not all the young man of the ghetto can see. Every day, as the years pass, and he becomes aware that there is nothing at the end of the road, he watches the rest of us go from peak to new peak of comfort. A few blocks away or in his television set, the young Negro of the slums sees the multiplying marvels of white America: more new cars and more summer vacations, more air-conditioned homes and neatly-kept lawns. But he cannot buy them.

He is told that Negroes are making progress. But what can that mean to him? He cannot experience the progress of others, nor should we seriously expect him to feel grateful because he is no longer a slave, or because he can vote, or eat at some lunch counters. He sees only the misery of his present and the darkening years ahead. Others tell him to work his way up as other minorities have done; and so he must. For he knows and we know, that only by his own efforts and his own labor will the Negro come to full equality.

But how is he to work: The jobs have fled to the suburbs or been replaced by machines, or have flown beyond the reach of those with limited education and skills. . . .

And thus, the black American youth is powerless to change his place or to make a better one for his children. He is denied the most fundamental of human needs: the need for identity, for recognition as a citizen and as a man. Here, and not in the pitiful charade of revolutionary oratory, is the breeding ground of reverse racism, and of aimless hostility and of violence. The violent youth of the ghetto is not simply protesting his condition, but making a destructive and self-defeating attempt to assert his worth and dignity as a human being, to tell us that though we may scorn his contribution, we must still respect his power.

Does all this give us direction for the future? I think it does. For the fact is that Americans are not cruel; or unjust or indifferent to suffering. The whole chronicle of our nation records the ultimate triumph of compassion and the spread of opportunity. Those are, and they remain, the basic instincts of the American people. And building on these noble sentiments, we know the way to a solution is open.

We have before us an historic opportunity. Out of the tension and trouble, out of our difficulty and danger, we can—and I believe we will—forge a new nation, better, stronger, more free and united than the country we had before. It is open to us now—it is demanded of us now, to engage in the great work of rebuilding our country. We can match our great unfulfilled needs—for housing and schools, roads and recreational facilities, public facilities and public services—with the hundreds of thousands of men and women, without jobs or in menial jobs, whose fury and frustration has wracked our cities these last four years. We can return hope while meeting the most urgent needs of the nation. We can build new cities—and a new community among men.

And let us not be discouraged by the legitimate question of resources; by those who ask where, in the face of a $30 billion war and fiscal crisis, we shall find the money for this kind of effort.

First, the most immediate need is for a national impact project: to put men to work, to restore possibility to the young and to give the resident of the ghetto some sense that the nation is committed to the fulfillment of his hopes. For such a program, over the months ahead, we can find the money in programs already authorized. We can slow down the race to the moon, if it means the salvation of our nation here on earth. We can postpone work on the supersonic transport, if it means that we can safely sit still in our cities. We can adjust our research and development programs, now running into the billions of dollars, if it allows us to search for purpose and human dignity within our communities.

Second, we can press our efforts for an early end to the war in Vietnam. This week's announcement, from Hanoi and Washington, seems to offer new hope that contacts leading to full-scale negotiations, will soon begin. Meanwhile we must encourage and accelerate efforts to return the major burden of the war to the South Vietnamese—where it should have been all along—and to lessen the cost, in American lives and money, for so long as the fighting continues.

Third, we must now commit ourselves to the proposition that as funds begin to be released from Vietnam, they will come home to the service of our domestic peace. We have to begin planning now the rebuilding effort to come. And if, from the outset, we seek the full participation of the people of the other America in this initial effort, then I believe they will understand, as we know, that everything cannot be done at once. They want not promises which cannot be met, but genuine commitment to achievable goals. We must make that commitment, and plan seriously for its fulfillment with them. That is a place to begin.

Let us, then, turn to our cities, where so much is promised, so much undone, so much threatened. There is work here for all—in the service of the most urgent public needs of the nation; work that will benefit white and black, fortunate and deprived, alike. City hospitals and school classrooms are overcrowded and out-dated everywhere; tens of thousands of young men and women cannot attend college because there simply is no room. In fact, the inventory is almost infinite: parks and playgrounds to be built, public facilities to be renovated, new transportation networks to be established, rivers and beaches to be cleansed of filth and again made fit for human use. And to all this must be added the demand of an expanding economy for a growing nation.

Now with all this to be done, let us stop thinking of the poor—the dropouts, the unemployed, those on welfare, and those who work for poverty wages—as liabilities. Let us see them for what they are: valuable resources, as people whose work can be directed to all these tasks to be done within our cities, and within the nation. . . .

≡ 15 ≡

The Art of Peace

THE UNITED STATES and the Soviet Union emerged from World War II as the two superpowers, capitalism and communism the two warring ideologies. In 1968, with its war against Vietnam increasingly condemned at home and abroad, the United States was discovering the limits of its superpower status. Old allies such as Britain and France refused to send troops to Vietnam to back up the Americans. As Kennedy says here, the United States had isolated itself through unilateralism. It had not shown that "decent respect for the opinions of mankind" hallowed in the Declaration of Independence. Kennedy recommends reaffirming America's commitment to the United Nations. He urges that America practice "the art of peace," as it did in his brother's administration in averting war during the Cuban missile crisis and achieving a Nuclear Test Ban Treaty.

For a decade after the escalations of 1965, the United States would continue at war with the small country of Vietnam. "Vietnam" stood in for "communism," which the war was meant to contain. What the North Vietnamese and Viet Cong were actually fighting for was not primarily communism but independence from foreign, particularly Western, domination. They had defeated the French, and now the Americans were fighting the same war, with new technology, more and bigger bombs, more troops. What the Americans were fighting for became less and less clear as the years went by. Pictures of Vietnamese wounded and dead—men, women, and children, young and old, civilian and soldier—fed the daily maw of horror. What abstract principle was this anti-communism that demanded that millions had to die?

In the face of the madness of full-blown war, one had to imagine a different reality. So Kennedy went back to his experience with an episode when the world, with his considerable help, chose peace instead of nuclear war.

In his book *Thirteen Days: A Memoir of the Cuban Missile Crisis,* RFK recounts a crucial moment, eleven days into the crisis, when he urged that President Kennedy employ a different strategy from what his brother's other advisers were suggesting. Soviet Premier Nikita Khrushchev had written two letters—the first being a more personal, emotional one about the fate of mankind, the second a formal, more hard-line one. The advisers were recommending a tough response to the second letter, but RFK suggested America answer the first and completely ignore the second. The president agreed, his letter was sent to Khrushchev, and the crisis began winding down.[1]

The Cuban missile crisis of October 1962 could have ended the world as we know it. In his foreword to *Thirteen Days*, Arthur

Schlesinger, Jr., notes that President Kennedy "took his negotiating credo from the British military analyst Basil Liddell Hart . . . : 'Keep strong, if possible. In any case, keep cool. Have unlimited patience. Never corner an opponent and always assist him to save face. Put yourself in his shoes—so as to see things through his eyes. Avoid self-righteousness like the devil—nothing is so self-blinding.'"[2]

SIGMA DELTA CHI JOURNALISM FRATERNITY
Ramada Inn, Portland, Oregon, April 17, 1968

At the height of the Cuban missile crisis of 1962, it became imperative to prevent the Soviets from flying nuclear warheads to Cuba. The range of their transport planes required that they stop and refuel on the way. The Republic of Guinea had the necessary airport facilities. The Soviets hoped to use them. The President of Guinea, Sékou Touré, was so critical of the United States that many Americans regarded him as a Communist and his country as "lost."

On the personal appeal of President Kennedy, President Touré nevertheless refused the Soviets permission to refuel in his country while carrying military cargoes. He did not do this because of anti-Communism. Nor did he do it because he had received great sums of American aid; he had not, and the Soviet Union had itself given assistance to Guinea. Nor was there any alliance or treaty between the United States and the Republic of Guinea. What had helped persuade Guinea of our deep sincerity was our understanding of her deep need for development and progress, recognized in our modest assistance program. It was our effort to understand Africa's desire to be heard in the councils of the world community. It was our effort to bring justice to black Americans at home—to affirm that African ancestry was no bar to full American citizenship. It was all of these things—and it was much more.

In the last analysis, what led Guinea to help us avert war in 1962 was a shared sense of what was right in relations between nations, a sense that an America which contributed its fair share to the quest for peace in the world deserved sympathy and support in a time of threat and danger to our own national security.

In short, America in 1962 did not go to war, because in this and other ways we had practiced the art of peace.

In this experience is a great lesson for the world and for America in 1968. America has become identified with power, and in that obsession we have forgotten our purposes. In truth, we are confronted by an extraordinary paradox. Our military strength and national wealth have multiplied beyond the wildest dreams of our fathers; yet the authority with which we speak, the respect in which we are held diminishes.

Only yesterday, a significant study was released which tells the depth of our problem. The annual survey of the Institute for Strategic Studies—an independent, highly respected research organization—concluded that while American power is growing steadily, American authority and influence in the world are declining. In the words of the survey: "The United States is richer and more powerful and perhaps more uncertain of herself than at any time since World War II." The world's respect for the liberal values of American society has been dimmed, and with that loss we have surrendered a dimension of our strength which is far beyond the measure of megatons.

There are two clear, inescapable reasons why American influence and prestige have seriously undermined our international position—our overcommitment in Vietnam and our undercommitment at home. The Institute report goes on to say: "The decline of American influence in West Europe and to a lesser extent Japan, India and Brazil spring from a sense that as America becomes more powerful, so the range of strategic interests which they share with her diminishes."

By the unilateral exercise of our overwhelming power, we isolated ourselves. To many of our traditional allies and neutral friends, we behaved as a Superpower ignoring our own historical commitment to a "decent respect for the opinions of mankind." The toughest guy in town can appoint himself sheriff and if he has enough ammunition he may keep the office for a long time, but his control will depend upon fear—and fear is not acceptable to us or the world as the basis of law and order. . . .

Our great strength—moral, political, economic, and military— must be used to seek peace with justice, to secure peace without fear. For those objectives, we must construct a foreign policy that will reassure the world of our judgment and our purposes. What are some of the elements of such a policy?

First is the need to recognize that we must accommodate difference and diversity both at home and abroad. The "monolithic" world of Communism has been shattered and compels us to recognize that the ancient force of nationalism is far stronger and enduring than the ideological power of Communist doctrine. We must learn, therefore, to deal with nations—whether in Southeast Europe or in Southeast Asia—as individual entities concerned with their own welfare and independence. . . .

Second, we must seek a more balanced and normal relationship with the Soviet Union. The Soviet Union, not a world movement but itself the second most powerful nation in the world, remains for us an unknown and dangerous adversary. The need for caution, however, cannot lead to a course of inaction. Russia is our rival, containing within her authoritarian system the continuing danger of conflict. But there is no reason why we should not seek out our parallel interests and attempt in every possible way to walk the path of friendship. We must seek those agreements, formal or informal, which will permit cooperation and reduce the danger of needless conflict. It is time to renew our dialogue, and explore every possibility for securing peace.

Third, we must recommit ourselves to the concept of the United Nations. . . . Certainly, the United Nations is an imperfect instrument, but it remains the best forum for the meeting of nations, where at the very least viewpoints can be exchanged and differences can be negotiated. It is appropriate and necessary that we know its weaknesses and work to strengthen its structure—but it is a hope of mankind and we must not ignore its possibilities.

Fourth, we must do everything within our power to halt the arms race. . . .

Fifth, we must reappraise the danger of China, accepting the need for that gigantic nation to take a more normal part in the international community. . . .

Finally, and most important, we must recognize that peace in the world means little to us unless we can preserve it at home.

We cannot continue to deny and postpone the demands of our own people, while spending billions in the name of freedom for others.

No nation can exert greater influence or power in the world than it can exercise over the streets of its own capital. No government can sustain international law and order unless it can do so at home.

No country can lead the fight for social justice unless its commitment to its own people is credible and determined—unless it seeks jobs and not the dole for its men, unless it feels anguish as long as any of its children are hungry, unless it believes in opportunity for all its citizens. Our future may lie beyond our vision, but it is not beyond our control.

Alfred Lord Tennyson once wrote: "The lights begin to twinkle from the rocks/ The long day wanes/ the low moon climbs/ the deep moans round with many voices./ Come, my friends, 'Tis not too late to seek a newer world."

I come to you today to ask your help in building that "newer world." With your support, with your commitment, with your confidence, we will do it.

16

Celebration in Brooklyn

RFK WAS BOTH idealist and realist. He liked to quote George Bernard Shaw: "Some men see things as they are, and ask why. I dream of things that never were, and ask why not." The dreaming gave him his vision of justice and peace; the "why not?" sent him tumbling back into the real world, where he worked to get results. His ideas about community involvement were novel at a time when the Democratic solution was more federal money for welfare programs, and the Republican solution was less federal money for welfare programs. RFK took ideas from both sides—care for the poor from Democrats, and business solutions from Republicans—and made something effective.

In the end, only one major corporation, IBM, built a plant in Bedford-Stuyvesant, bringing in 400 jobs. The Bedford-Stuyvesant Restoration Corporation continues to this day with its mission "to improve the quality of life for all residents of the Bedford-Stuyvesant area of Brooklyn by strengthening the local economy, family life and culture through a wide variety of programs and

services in business development, the arts, youth education, housing and computer training."[1] Evan Thomas concludes that "over
time, the corporation became, relatively speaking, a success. It did
not transform Bedford-Stuyvesant into a middle-class neighborhood, but it did loosen up mortgage money from white-owned
banks and helped create a stock of decent housing."[2] "Decent"was
a word Robert Kennedy was using a lot that spring of 1968, and I
think the achievement of a "stock of decent housing" is considerable. Perhaps most importantly, Robert Kennedy's idea for
Bedford-Stuyvesant has become the model for thousands of inner-
city community development corporations around the country.[3]

Bed-Stuy has become a vibrant neighborhood, and one of its
most celebrated sons, Spike Lee, shoots many of his films there.
As I write this, the Bedford-Stuyvesant Restoration Corporation is
celebrating its fortieth anniversary with events like an all-day RFK
Memorial Holiday Party on Restoration Plaza.[4]

BEDFORD-STUYVESANT, NEW YORK
April 18, 1968

The announcement that IBM will locate a plant facility in
Bedford-Stuyvesant is further evidence of the capacity of the
community to control its own destiny—and I greet this announcement with appreciation and enthusiasm.

I have appreciation for IBM—for by this decision they have
demonstrated confidence in Bedford-Stuyvesant and faith in the

potential economic growth of the community. The new plant—the first major industrial facility to be located in Bedford-Stuyvesant—will occupy an eight-story building at the corner of Gates and Nostrand Avenue. It will provide jobs for the people in the community—for IBM plans to employ more than 300 workers there by the end of 1969. And the training these men and women receive in the most advanced technology will enable them to contribute not just to their own livelihood but to the life of the community. In the new plant they will work producing computer cables that will be used in IBM products around the world.

I have enthusiasm for all the people of Bedford-Stuyvesant—and for the Restoration Corporation. For the decision made by IBM is surely a tribute to the efforts this community has made to bring together private and public energy to rebuild their neighborhood. By initiating a broad range of community projects, the people of Bedford-Stuyvesant have made clear their conviction that cooperation and mutual understanding can bring results and improve conditions in their city. And now one of our great corporations has decided that Bedford-Stuyvesant can be a thriving home for industry—that it is good business to contribute their expertise and resources to the community and bring the community into their operation.

In this way a community grows and prospers—and that means its people prosper as well. So we should all congratulate IBM for its foresight, and we should all recognize that it is the people of Bedford-Stuyvesant who prompted this act of faith in their future.

IBM has taken the first step. We should expect that other companies will follow their example—bringing their particular expertise into the community, providing more jobs and varied training programs. For together—each individual and each company and each level of government—we can attack the problems that seem so overwhelming, and we can master them.

17

Ending Hunger and Malnutrition

Tʜɪs ꜱɪᴍᴘʟᴇ ꜱᴛᴀᴛᴇᴍᴇɴᴛ calls on the medical profession, private industry, farmers, government, and people in general to work together to end hunger and malnutrition in America. In 1968, there were 14.5 million Americans going hungry. Nearly forty years later, the number had risen to 35 million.[1]

Sᴛᴀᴛᴇᴍᴇɴᴛ ᴏꜰ Rᴏʙᴇʀᴛ F. Kᴇɴɴᴇᴅʏ
ᴏɴ ᴛʜᴇ Rᴇᴘᴏʀᴛ ᴏꜰ ᴛʜᴇ Cɪᴛɪᴢᴇɴꜱ' Bᴏᴀʀᴅ
ᴏꜰ IɴQᴜɪʀʏ ɪɴᴛᴏ Hᴇᴀʟᴛʜ ᴀɴᴅ Nᴜᴛʀɪᴛɪᴏɴ
ɪɴ ᴛʜᴇ Uɴɪᴛᴇᴅ Sᴛᴀᴛᴇꜱ
Tuesday, April 23, 1968

Yesterday a distinguished panel of private citizens called on the nation to use its resources to bring nutritional food to 14.5 million Americans who do not get enough to eat. . . .

This Board—composed of leading doctors, ministers, lawyers and experts in nutritional health—confirmed what many officials had expected, but what most Americans find hard to believe:

- That in the United States, the richest nation in the world, children die in infancy because their mothers cannot afford to buy milk.
- That thousands of American children suffer from permanent brain damage and are mentally retarded for life because their diet does not include enough protein and vitamins.
- That thousands of children cannot learn their lessons because they go to school without breakfast, cannot afford to buy lunch in school and return home to a supper without meat or green vegetables or milk.
- That thousands of old people are compelled to subsist entirely on liquids because they lack enough money to get a decent meal.

This finding, documented with details and pictures, constitutes a national disgrace—we are presented with the hard reality of a national crisis, and we are challenged to respond promptly and effectively.

The richest country in the world must be able to afford to feed its hungry people. The most prosperous society on the globe must be able to save its children from death, disease and despair that result from a lack of adequate food.

I believe that no task should stand higher on our national agenda. I call on all Americans—on the medical profession, on private industry, on the farmers, on government, and on all individuals to respond to the plight of these millions who are hungry.

I call on the medical profession to help by training doctors and nurses to recognize malnutrition as the cause of many disabling diseases. I call on hospitals to keep records and perform tests on their patients to detect the presence of malnutrition.

I call on private industry to develop their domestic markets in healthy foods, like fortified soft drinks and cereals, so that these products are more readily available to those who desperately need them.

I call on farmers to direct their produce toward those Americans in need of food assistance—and I call on government to use funds allocated for food aid to pay the farmers who produce food for hungry Americans. Last year $500 million allocated by Congress to purchase food for those in need was returned to the Treasury because the Secretary of Agriculture refused to spend it. With millions of Americans going to bed without supper, these funds must be used—and used effectively.

I call on government at all levels to expand programs of food assistance. When our nation is faced with the crisis described by the Citizens' Board, it is intolerable that government efforts to provide food through school lunch, commodity distribution and food stamp programs are helping only 18 percent of those who need aid—1,400,000 fewer people than participated in these programs six years ago.

I call on every American to ask himself how he might join in a common effort to end hunger and malnutrition. We should send Care packages to starving people in Mississippi and Alaska and to migrant workers in California and New Jersey as well as to people in need around the globe.

There can be no delay to our action. The Citizens' Board has demonstrated the problem with dramatic clarity. Now we must respond—all of us—so that no American suffers from hunger any longer.

18

No More Vietnams

O N April 24, Kennedy took on the war again. He noted that the introduction of American troops into the internal affairs of another nation usually "transformed a factional struggle into a nationalist struggle against foreign domination." He urged that America reach out to its allies in Europe. He noted that the war took precious resources from solving domestic problems, weakening the state of the union.

Indiana University

Bloomington, Indiana, April 24, 1968

Long ago it was said, "The time for taking a lesson from history is ever at hand for those that are wise." The war in Vietnam is not yet finally consigned to history. The fighting and bloodshed continue. The bombing of North Vietnam is restricted; but that too continues. And the negotiations, toward which we have taken the most tentative and still far from certain steps—these have not yet begun.

Still in one sense the war may be passing into history; and that is in the thinking of the American people. There has been settled, in the year 1968, one simple proposition: the American people—scholars and officials, soldiers and citizens, students and parents—are determined that there must not be another Vietnam.

What we must now debate and come to understand is what it is about—the war in Vietnam that we are determined not to repeat; what effect this determination will have on our own policies and goals; what it means to our own lives and to the future of our nation. What does it mean to say, No more Vietnams?

It is sometimes asserted that Vietnam is "the battlefield where we must make the decision which may well determine the future shape of Asia." But it is unlikely that whatever the outcome of the war in Vietnam, the dominoes will fall in either direction. . . .

Communism was destroyed in Indonesia in 1965 with terrible slaughter by the people of Indonesia themselves. . . . Cambodia, under the leadership of Prince Sihanouk, has sought neutrality in its foreign policy but acted strongly and successfully against any internal Communist activity. . . .

Almost all the nations of Asia and Africa are only recently emerged from colonial domination—from 300 years in which the entire structure of their societies and culture was torn apart, degraded, and humiliated. They are still torn today by the tremendous effort to modernize and develop their economies; to create new leadership groups capable of managing modern society and to cope with demands for social justice that have been awakened by the example of the successful egalitarian West. We can expect that these nations and the nations of Latin America, which are Western but not yet modern, will be plagued by instability for decades to come.

For these nations we can hope that their progress will be humane and decent; hope that they avoid the excesses of violence which accompanied the development of so many nations of the West. And we should offer to their effort such assistance as we can, or what will be effective.

But we cannot continue, as we too often have done in the past, to automatically identify the United States with the preservation of a particular internal order within those countries, or confuse our own national interest with the rule of a particular faction within them. Of course, those in power in these countries will often seek to preserve their position by requesting our help.

Faced with such requests, we must make calm and discriminating judgments as to which governments can and should be helped, which are moving effectively to defend themselves and meet the needs of their people. Where the central interests of the United States are not directly threatened, I could propose a simple functional test: We should give no more assistance to a government against any internal threat than that government is capable of using itself, through its agencies and instruments. We can help them but we cannot again try to do their jobs for them.

. . . But let us understand the full significance of the limitation I suggest. It does not prevent us from aiding any nation against truly external aggression. It does not prevent us from extending reasonable assistance to developing nations. It does prevent us from taking over an internal struggle from a minority government or a government too ineffective or corrupt to gain the support of its own people. It would allow the future of each country to be settled, essentially, by the people of that country. . . .

The worst thing we could do would be to take as our mission the suppression of disorder and internal upheaval everywhere it appears. This is even more true if the means for this policeman's role is to be the indiscriminate introduction of American troops into the internal struggles of other nations.

Their presence can transform a factional struggle within a country into a nationalist struggle against foreign domination. Their introduction commits our prestige to the outcome of diverse struggles we may barely understand. It may lead the government and the people to refuse essential sacrifices. Most ironic of all, ill-considered military intervention may well increase the very communist influence they are aimed to prevent; for communism has gained its greatest strength when allied with the national reaction to foreign intervention, invasion, or colonial domination. . . .

America was a great force in the world, with immense prestige, long before we became a great military power. That power has come to us and we cannot renounce it, but neither can we afford to forget that the real constructive force in the world comes not from bombs, but from imaginative ideas, warm sympathies, and a generous spirit. These are qualities that cannot be manufactured by specialists in public relations. They are the natural qualities of a people pursuing decency and human dignity in its own undertakings without arrogance or hostility or delusions of superiority toward others; a people whose ideals for others are firmly rooted in the realities of the society we have built for ourselves.

≡ **19** ≡

Health Care

Since 1948, when Harry Truman proposed universal health insurance, Democrats have tried to bring the idea to fruition. In this next speech, Kennedy pledged to do it: "I think this nation is willing to make the effort necessary for an effective system of care. We have the resources to do it—we have the will to do it—and we are going to do it if I am the next President of the United States." Today, after nearly four decades in which war and cold war expenditures have trumped investment in social services, we're still not there. Forty-seven million Americans, 15 percent of the population, have no health insurance. That's down from 54 million in 1968, but still "unacceptable," as RFK liked to say.

In 1994, President Bill Clinton and Hillary Clinton tried to create a program of national health insurance to cover every American, but got ambushed by the insurance lobby. Ten years later, RFK's brother, Senator Edward Kennedy, introduced his Health Security and Affordability Act. His remarks could have been uttered by his brother in the 1968 campaign:

". . . The failure to enact universal health insurance is an ongoing American tragedy. Today, 44 million Americans have no health insurance, an increase of four million in just two years. In the course of this year, 73 million—one in every three Americans under 65—will go without coverage for an extended period of time. Soaring costs are pricing health care out of the reach of individuals and employers alike. Every year, more and more firms cut back on coverage or cancel it altogether. . . .

"The history of America is in large measure the history of the struggle to assert the public interest over the special interests. Whether the challenge was to end monopoly power, or guarantee a minimum wage, or enact Social Security and Medicare, the public interest—the people's interest—ultimately prevailed over the interests of the wealthy and powerful, and that's what has made our country good as well as great. This is no time to turn back, or give up in the long battle for health care for all. After years of debate, we know the issue and we know the importance of dealing fairly with the challenge. We have it in our power to make the fundamental right to health care a reality for all Americans. I say let's get it done—if not this year, then next year with a new Congress and a new Administration elected with a mandate to get it done. . . ."[1]

INDIANA UNIVERSITY MEDICAL SCHOOL
Indianapolis, Indiana, April 26, 1968

I want to speak with you today about a national dilemma; one which affects not just the poor, or the Negro, but those within the mainstream of American life. It is the problem of health care—what it costs, how effective it is, what it will be like in the future.

For the grim fact is that across the nation, the condition of American health care is grave—and in parts of the nation, it is critical. We confront the intolerable conditions, attributable not to any act of God, but to the neglect and indifference of man. "If we believe men have any personal rights at all," Aristotle said, "then they must have an absolute moral right to such a measure of good health as society alone can provide."

In the last decade, the United States has moved toward making this "absolute moral right" more of a reality for all of our citizens. We have in the Federal Government erected a vast web of programs—more than 200 in one agency alone—to supply better health care for Americans. In just two years—between 1965 and 1967—national health expenditures rose from $39 billion to $47 billion, and the Government's share of that cost climbed from 25 to 35 percent. Within a decade—by 1975—we will be spending more than $100 billion in health care, and almost half of this enormous expense will be borne by the Federal Government—through programs ranging from VA hospitals to Medicare and Medicaid expenses. Yet the key question—as with any massive Government effort—is not how much we have spent; not how many programs have begun; but what we have bought for our efforts.

In the field of health, the answer to this question is not a happy one. For despite these billions of dollars and hundreds of programs, the national system of health care has failed to meet the most urgent needs of millions of Americans. . . .

In fact, even today, the average hospital cost for the 30 million Americans who will need such care this year—not costly doctors' fees and special services—will be $566 more than the average American worker earns in a month. Indeed for these people the problem may be more than for the poor—who at least get some kind of care, however inadequate. But the 54 million Americans lacking any hospital insurance, with 61 million Americans lacking surgical insurance—and with more than 100 million Americans lacking protection against major illness—the typical American worker may soon find his life savings drained away by a single stroke of fate. The issue before us, then, is simple: Shall we continue to watch as medical costs soar beyond the reach of most Americans, condemning the poor to illness and the average American to the whim of fate—or are we going to act to make decent medical care something more than a luxury of the affluent?

I think what we want is clear. And I think this nation is willing to make the effort necessary for an effective system of care. We have the resources to do it—we have the will to do it—and we are going to do it if I am the next President of the United States. To accomplish this task, we must understand that the root problem is one of structure—one which goes to the heart of our method of delivering health care. We are pumping billions of dollars of new money into the health industry—but without the slightest effort to change the existing system; a system under which people are cared for in the costliest of institutions, the hospital, by the costliest of manpower, the doctor. And here, in the crux of our crisis, the poor who have no access to care, and the middle income family who increasingly cannot afford it—their dilemma is part of the inefficient structure of health care that we have tried to subsidize without reforming.

No program to improve the nation's health will be effective unless we understand the conditions of injustice which underlie disease. It is illusory to think we can cure a sickly child—and ignore his need for enough food to eat. It is foolish to pour in money to cure the effect of filth-ridden slums—without acting to eradicate the slums that breed so much disease. It is pointless to establish community health projects to cure the ills of mind and body—if we do not understand that a community of the jobless, the hopeless, the purposeless spawns disease in the minds and bodies of its victims. We will not really cure the pathology of individuals unless we begin to come to grips with the pathology of these communities.

Education, jobs, community participation, an end to hunger, these are the elements of a healthy citizenry. And they must be achieved. For it is neither economical nor compassionate to care for the consequences of poverty, and ignore its roots.

As this is true for communities of poverty, so the need for broad action is true for the whole society. All of our efforts to combat cancer may be—as one noted doctor put it—less important than the single step of reducing the number of children who become cigarette smokers.

All our programs to train new doctors may not mean as much to the health of our city as forceful action to eliminate the pollution of our air. All our emergency rooms will not ease the pain of auto accident victims as much as effective controls on unsafe drivers and unsafe cars.

. . . These steps are not easy. But they can be taken—in Washington, yes, but more important, within our communities by concerned, committed citizens. And above all, it is for you, members of the medical profession, to lead the way—taking as your motto, the words of Albert Einstein, who said: "Concern for man himself and his fate must always be the chief interest of all technical endeavors. . . . in order that the creations of our mind shall be a blessing and not a curse to mankind."

That is the task before us. With your help, that is the task we shall achieve.

According to Arthur Schlesinger, Jr., there was perfunctory applause after the speech. "A black janitor called from the balcony, 'We want Kennedy.' On the floor, students shouted back, 'No we don't.' Someone asked where the money for Kennedy's health program would come from. Looking at the incipient MDs about to enter lucrative careers, he snapped, 'From you.'" Then:

Let me say something about the tone of these questions. I look around this room and I don't see many black faces who will become doctors. You can talk about where the money will come from. . . . Part of civilized society is to let people go to medical school who come from ghettos. You don't see many people coming out of the ghettos or off the Indian reservations to medical school. You are the privileged ones. . . . It's our society, not just our government, that spends twice as much on pets as on the poverty program. It's the poor who carry the major burden in Vietnam. You sit here as white medical students, while black people carry the burden of the fighting in Vietnam.[2]

▤ **20** ▤

The American Farmland

O N APRIL 27, Vice President Hubert Horatio Humphrey threw his hat into the presidential ring. Before he became vice president, Humphrey represented Minnesota in the Senate and was a favorite of the liberal wing of the Democratic Party. In 1960 John Kennedy had defeated him in the Democratic presidential primaries. As Lyndon Johnson's vice president, Humphrey became a fervent defender of Johnson's escalations of the Vietnam war, and by doing so he lost his liberal constituency. In 1968, a time made tragic by war and the assassination of Martin Luther King, Humphrey declared that his campaign would embody "the politics of joy." Because he had waited so long to declare, Humphrey was ineligible for any of the primaries, and those who wanted to vote for him had to select a surrogate on the ballot; in Indiana, that was Governor Roger Branigan.

The Indiana primary was May 7, and though it was a conservative state, Kennedy won it, with 41 percent of the vote; Branigan received 31 and McCarthy 27.

"There was a kind of sweetness to Kennedy's Nebraska campaign," writes Evan Thomas. In Indiana, he had been "wildly cheered by angry blacks, then cheered with equal enthusiasm by blue-collar whites who professed to hate blacks." Now, although he was from the East and manifestly not a farmer, he was connecting on a human level with another group of people whose lives were hard, in the small farm towns of the Great Plains. "He would joke that he came from the 'great farm state of New York,' and when a gust of wind blew away a piece of paper on which he had scribbled some notes, he quipped, 'There goes my farm program.'"[1]

But actually he had much more, as the following speeches demonstrate.

On May 14, Kennedy won the Nebraska primary by even wider margins than in Indiana: 51.5 percent to McCarthy's 31. If you looked at the records of the two senators, there were few differences, but where they differed was in what Schlesinger calls "values," with McCarthy appealing to suburban whites, and Kennedy to "the disestablished and unrepresented."[2]

Richard Harwood of the *Washington Post* wrote, "We discovered in 1968, this deep, almost mystical bond that existed between Robert Kennedy and the Other America. It was a disquieting experience for reporters. . . . We were forced to recognize in Watts [California] and Gary [Indiana] and Chimney Rock [Nebraska] that the real stake in the American political process involved not the fate of speech-writers and fund-raisers but the lives of millions of people seeking hope out of despair."[3]

McCarthy, meanwhile, was becoming increasingly bitter, refusing to congratulate Kennedy for his wins in Indiana and Nebraska.[4]

OTOE COUNTY COURTHOUSE
Nebraska City, Nebraska, May 10, 1968

. . . Nearly half our Nation's poor—some 14 million Americans—live in rural areas. . . . According to any measure, rural America has grave problems. Infant mortality is far higher among the rural poor than among the most deprived in our cities. One in four rural homes is substandard compared with one in seven in urban areas. Rural unemployment is about 18%, while unemployment nationally is about 4%. Rural areas have half as many doctors for their people as the rest of the nation, and 1/3 the number of nurses. The percentage of rural teachers not properly certified is twice as high as in urban areas.

We must make rural America live again. This will involve not only bringing a fair return to the farmer for his product, but bringing industry and needed social services to rural areas. We have already lost too much of the value and stability—the very backbone of America—that is the quality of rural life. A new American commitment to our rural areas is in order.

During this campaign and previously, I have made a number of proposals to aid the development and revitalization of rural life:

- proposals to raise farm income and help the small farmer and the young farmer particularly;
- a program of tax incentives to encourage industry to locate in rural poverty areas and provide employment for their residents;
- increased federal assistance for building of the roads and airports and schools and water and sewer facilities that rural America must have if it is to develop according to its potential.

But there is a further dimension to the effort. A comprehensive program to end rural poverty must also involve a tremendous increase in the supply of social services that people need if they are to share fully in America's great wealth. The provision of these services is essential not only for economic development but in order to provide thousands of employment opportunities that are simply not available for the young men and women who now stream forth from the towns and farms of our nation to large cities in search of employment opportunities that are simply not available in the areas where they grew up. We can create new career opportunities in rural America which will not only avoid forcing people to leave their home communities if they do not wish to, but offer help in alleviating poverty and in providing adequate community social services. . . .

BROOKINGS, SOUTH DAKOTA
May 11, 1968

I come before you as a man of the East—as one who has lived most of his life in or near large cities. But I am also here as an American—as one who believes that when one of us prospers, all of us prosper; and when one falters, so do we all.

. . . We know too, I think, what the stakes are. It is not simply economic well-being—it is the survival of the enduring values of diversity in America, the fight against the loss of diverse ways of life, the battle to prevent America's farms from becoming factories producing bland food and bland men, driving our citizens into homogenous cities, distinguished from each other only by the poisons in their air.

. . . In my judgment, the need for adequate food here in the United States is a key to agricultural America's survival. I have proposed in the past that we at last make a thorough survey of hunger in America—and that, once we grasp the depth of the problem—for the present and the future—we begin to plan a farm policy which promotes production to provide a decent diet for Americans.

This is in no sense a proposal for a dole—although clearly those who cannot feed themselves cannot be permitted to starve. Instead it recognizes that men who now lack any jobs at all are men who cannot feed their families—and that, with a vigorous program to bring employment into urban and rural America, the demand for satisfying, nutritious food will greatly increase. Thus, if we plan to provide jobs for all, we also plan for a vital, productive role in the future for America's farmers. . . .

For it is no parochial task to attempt to improve life within rural America. It is instead the same task as the rebuilding of our cities—the preservation of our natural resources—the cleansing of our air and water.

It is the task of giving to Americans the widest possible opportunity to make what they will of their own lives—to expand the limits of human freedom and action—to preserve what is valuable and improve what needs changing. . . .

≡ 21 ≡

The Question of Welfare

Kennedy had been wrestling with the problems of public welfare since he entered the Senate in 1965. The question of welfare is essentially a question of children, and Kennedy's love of children, all ten of his own (and an eleventh on the way) and all others, seems to have been unconditional and absolute. Of course, children can't vote, so their rights and their well-being are secondary in the calculations of most politicians. A month before he died, when asked how he would like to be remembered, he replied: "Something about the fact that I made some contribution to either my country, or those who were less well off. I think again back to what Camus wrote about the fact that perhaps this world is a world in which children suffer, but we can lessen the number of suffering children, and if you do not do this, then who will do this? I'd like to feel that I'd done something to lessen that suffering."[1]

Peter Edelman was an aide to RFK and helped craft the senator's thoughts about welfare. Later he worked in the Clinton administration, and resigned in protest over Clinton's support of the 1996 welfare reform bill, which ended six decades of federal help to poor children. In a way extending the thought of Robert Kennedy into the 21st century, Edelman wrote in 2003: "'Welfare' is the wrong issue anyway. Reducing the number of people on welfare is laudable only if it results in making people better off. Ending poverty and achieving a better shake for all of those in difficulty even amid record prosperity are the right goals. Welfare—cash assistance for people at the bottom—is only a small part of a strategy to pursue those goals. But it should not be a dirty word. We need it to help when the economy goes sour either nationally or locally, and for people who are not in a position to work outside the home. It should be a safety net."[2]

PRESS RELEASE
Los Angeles, California, May 19, 1968

Perhaps the area of our greatest domestic failure is in the system of welfare—public assistance to those in need. There is a deep sense of dissatisfaction, among recipient and government alike—about what welfare has become over the last thirty years, and where it seems to be going.

Welfare is many things to many people. To the recipient it may be the difference between life and starvation, between a house and homelessness, between the cold wind and a child's coat. To the taxpayer—facing inflation in the cost of living, paying for his home and educating his children—welfare may be an unwarranted imposition on an already overburdened tax bill. To certain politicians, willing to oversimplify and confuse the issue, it may be a means to easy popularity.

The bill is rising further everyday.

With all this enormous expenditure, might we not expect that the recipients would be satisfied? Yet the fact is that they are not. They are as dissatisfied with the welfare system as is anyone in the U.S. Is this rank ingratitude—or is it an indication of how the welfare system has failed? For what are we to make of a system which seems to satisfy neither giver nor recipient—which embitters all those who come in contact with it? . . .

Welfare began as a necessary program of assistance for those unable to work. But we have tried as well to make it the easy answer to the complex, but by no means insurmountable, problem of unemployment. Our society is full of men without work: two and a half million who can find only part-time or occasional jobs; over half a million more who have become so discouraged that they no longer even look for work; and—especially in the black ghettoes of the great cities—hundreds of thousands who have dropped from sight, without homes or families, unseen by all the computers and agencies of government.

These are men like other men. They marry and have children; or they do not marry, but have children just the same. In either case, they often leave home under the strain of joblessness and poverty. We have dealt with the resulting female-headed families not by putting the men to work but by giving the mothers and children welfare. They might have wanted fathers and husbands; we have given them checks. In fact, the welfare system itself has created many of these fatherless families—by requiring the absence of a father as a condition for receiving aid; no one will ever know how many left their families to let them qualify for assistance so that they might eat, or find a place to live.

More basically, welfare itself has done much to divide our people, to alienate us one from the other. Partly this separation comes from the understandable resentment of the taxpayer, helplessly watching your welfare rolls and your property taxes rise. But there is greater resentment among the poor, the recipient of our charity. Some of it comes from the brutality of the welfare system itself: from the prying bureaucrat, an all-powerful administrator deciding at his desk who is deserving and who is not, who shall live another month and who may starve next week.

But the root problem is in the fact of dependency and uselessness itself. Unemployment means having nothing to do—which means nothing to do with the rest of us. To be without work, to be without use to one's fellow citizens, is to be in truth the Invisible Man of whom Ralph Ellison wrote; as John Adams said a century and a half ago, "the poor man's conscience is clear, yet he is ashamed. . . . He feels himself out of the sight of others, groping in the dark Mankind takes no notice of him. He rambles and wanders unheeded. In the midst of a crowd, at church, in the market . . . he is in as much obscurity as he would be in a garret or a cellar. He is not disapproved, censured, or reproached: he is only not seen." Well might we conclude with Adams that "To be wholly overlooked, and to know it, is intolerable." So we have seen—all over the country.

We often quote Lincoln's warning that America could not survive half slave and half free. Nor can it survive while millions of our people are slaves to dependency and poverty, waiting on the favor of their fellow citizens to write them checks. Fellowship, community, shared patriotism—these essential values of our civilization do not come from just buying and consuming goods together. They come from a shared sense of individual independence and personal effort. They come from working together to build a country—that is the answer to the welfare crisis.

The answer to the welfare crisis is work, jobs, self-sufficiency, and family integrity; not a massive new extension of welfare; not a great new outpouring of guidance counselors to give the poor more advice. We need jobs, dignified employment at decent pay; the kind of employment that lets a man say to his community, to his family, to his country, and most important, to himself, "I helped to build this country. I am a participant in its great public ventures. I am a man.". . .

≡ 22 ≡

The New Politics

1 968 WAS THE YEAR of a politics of change—the so-called New Politics—a politics of citizen participation, of overturning old ways of doing things and even old governments—and RFK did much to define it. In this speech given in San Francisco, he praised the intensity of citizen participation—students and teachers, housewives and professionals, blue collar and white collar— in the electoral process in 1968. Finally, he said, "What the new politics is, in the last analysis, is a reaffirmation of the best within the great political traditions of our nation: compassion for those who suffer, determination to right the wrongs within our nation, and a willingness to think and to act anew, free from old concepts and false illusions."

RFK's politics was a mixture of old and new. As Evan Thomas notes, perhaps too cynically, "Much was later made of the 'new politics' of the Robert Kennedy campaign. [Kennedy aide Adam] Walinsky proclaimed the new age on day one: 'Our strategy is to change the rules of nominating a president. . . . We're going to do it a new way. In the streets.'" But it was a two-pronged strategy, says Thomas: As Walinsky was "declaring a people's crusade, Kennedy was telling columnist Jimmy Breslin that the boss of old-fashioned bosses, Mayor Richard Daley of Chicago, was the key to victory."[1]

Peter Edelman has contrasted RFK with New Democrats like Bill Clinton and Al Gore, calling Kennedy "the first 'new' Democrat, the first to espouse values of grassroots empowerment and express doubts about big bureaucratic approaches, the first to call for partnerships between the private and public sectors and insist that what we now call civic renewal is essential, the first to put particular emphasis on personal responsibility. But Robert Kennedy differed from those who now call themselves 'new' Democrats because he also insisted on national policy, national leadership, and national funding to help empower people at the bottom and address other pressing issues. His work and his views were prescient. It is still not too late to learn from them."[2]

PRESS GANG LUNCHEON
San Francisco, California, May 21, 1968

Perhaps it is true that there is nothing new under the sun; but that is only in the longest view of man and his history. It is clear by now that 1968 will go down as the year the new politics of the next decade or more began. It is the year when the existing political wisdom had proven unable to cope with the turbulence of our times, inspire our young people, or provide answers to problems we face as a nation. And therefore this is the year when the old politics must be a thing of the past.

But if this is true—and I profoundly believe that it is—then there is no more important question than what the new politics is. What are its components, and what does it mean to the future of the country?

The most obvious element of the new politics is the politics of citizen participation, of personal involvement. Of course Americans have always participated in their political life, and worked in political campaigns. What is different about 1968 is the extent and quality of that work. People—students and teachers, housewives and professionals—have worked not just in the primary states, but in precinct caucuses and county conventions; seeking not to serve the candidate selected by the party machinery, but to exercise democratic choice. Beyond this, they have engaged hundreds of thousands, perhaps millions, of their fellow-citizens in a face-to-face discussion and debate, not just about the merits of one or another candidate, but about the substantive issues which are at the heart of the election.

The next priority for change—the first element of a new politics for the United States—is in our policy toward the world. Too much and for too long, we have acted as if our great military might and wealth could bring about an American solution to every world problem. . . .

We must be willing to recognize that the world is changing, and that our greatest potential ally is the simple and enduring fact that men want to be free and independent. . . .

The second demand of the new politics is here at home. It begins with the recognition that federal spending will not solve all our problems, and that money cannot buy dignity, self-respect, or fellow feeling between citizens.

The new politics will recognize that these things do come from working together to build a country; and it will make the first domestic task of the next administration the creation of dignified jobs, at decent pay, for all those who can and want to work. It will be for a far better public assistance system, one which affords adequate help to those who cannot work, without the indignities and random cruelties which afflict the present welfare systems. . . .

The third element of the new politics is to halt and reverse the growing accumulation of power and authority in the central government in Washington, and to return that power of decision to the American people in their own local communities. For the truth is that with all the good that has been accomplished over the last thirty years—by unemployment compensation, Medicare, and fair labor standards, by the programs for education, housing, and community development—for all that, still the truth is that too often the programs have been close to failures.

If this is to change—and it must change—we must recognize that the answer is not just another federal program, another department or administration, another layer of bureaucracy in Washington. The real answer is in the full involvement of the private enterprise system—in the creation of jobs, the building of housing, the provision of services, in training and education and health care. Through a flexible and comprehensive system of tax incentives, we can and should encourage private enterprise to devote its energies and resources to these great social tasks, which I believe [it] could help us to accomplish with far less cost, far more effectiveness, and far more freedom than with more government programs. . . .

Finally, the new politics of 1968 has a final need: and that is an end to some of the clichés and stereotypes of past political rhetoric. In too much of our political dialogue, "liberals" have been those who wanted to spend more money, while "conservatives" have been those who wanted to pretend that all problems should solve themselves. Emerson once wrote that "conservatism makes no poetry, breathes no prayer, has no invention; it is all memory," while reform, he wrote, "has no gratitude, no prudence, no husbandry."

But the times are too difficult, our needs are too great, for such restricted visions. There is nothing "liberal" about a constant expansion of the federal government, stripping citizens of their public power—the right to share in the government of affairs— that was the founding purpose of this nation. There is nothing conservative about standing idle while millions of fellow citizens lose their lives and their hopes, while their frustration turns to fury that tears the fabric of society and freedom.

[Franklin Delano] Roosevelt once told us that "the system of party responsibility in America requires a . . . liberal party and a conservative party" and so it is today. We have no need—indeed, we cannot afford—to blur distinctions and eliminate differences, until the people are left with no dialogue and no choice except the pleasure of a candidate's smile. What we do need, and what 1968 must bring, is a better liberalism and a better conservatism. We need a liberalism, in its wish to do good, that yet recognizes the limits to rhetoric and American power abroad; that knows the answer to all problems is not spending money; that is willing to accomplish its great ends by trusting the American people themselves, and not by seeking the constant expansion of federal authority. We need a conservatism, in its wish to preserve the enduring values of the American society, that yet recognizes the urgent need to bring opportunity to all citizens, that is willing to take action to meet the needs of the future.

What the new politics is, in the last analysis, is a reaffirmation of the best within the great political traditions of our nation: compassion for those who suffer, determination to right the wrongs within our nation, and a willingness to think and to act anew, free from old concepts and false illusions.

That is the kind of politics—that is the kind of leadership—the American people want.

☰ 23 ☰

Cleaning Our Air and Our Waters

IN THIS TEXT, DATED two years before the first Earth Day and anticipating the global environmental movement, Kennedy addresses the care of the earth. Decades later, his son Robert F. Kennedy, Jr., who has made environmental activism his lifework, wrote, "George W. Bush will go down in history as America's worst environmental president. In a ferocious three-year attack, the Bush administration has initiated more than 200 major rollbacks of America's environmental laws, weakening the protection of our country's air, water, public lands and wildlife. Cloaked in meticulously crafted language designed to deceive the public, the administration intends to eliminate the nation's most important environmental laws by the end of the year. . . .

"Today, George W. Bush and his court are treating our country as a grab bag for the robber barons, doling out the commons to large polluters. Last year, as the calamitous rollbacks multiplied, the corporate-owned TV networks devoted less than four percent of their news minutes to environmental stories. If they knew the truth, most Americans would share my fury that this president is allowing his corporate cronies to steal America from our children."[1]

In the forty years since 1968, there have been environmental victories on a small scale. The health of the Hudson River, championed by many, including RFK, Jr. and Pete Seeger, has improved.

But there is now a greater environmental crisis than pollution: Global warming has become the worst threat to humanity since nuclear weapons. RFK's press release from May 26, 1968, is prescient: "In Los Angeles County, the health threat caused by air pollution due to automobile fumes is such that doctors advise more than 10,000 persons each year to move out of the area." Those automobile fumes went right up into the atmosphere and contributed to the greenhouse gases that are melting the polar ice caps and threatening life as we know it.

Since the early 1990s, Al Gore has been the major voice in elucidating the threat and showing a way out. A brief excerpt from a 2006 Gore speech outlines a problem that we might not need to be dealing with if RFK had lived.

"A few days ago, scientists announced alarming new evidence of the rapid melting of the perennial ice of the north polar cap, continuing a trend of the past several years that now confronts us with the prospect that human activities, if unchecked in the next decade, could destroy one of the earth's principle mechanisms for cooling itself. Another group of scientists presented evidence that human activities are responsible for the dramatic warming of sea surface temperatures in the areas of the ocean where hurricanes form. A few weeks earlier, new information from yet another team showed dramatic increases in the burning of forests throughout the American West, a trend that has increased decade by decade, as warmer temperatures have dried out soils and vegetation. All these findings come at the end of a summer with record breaking temperatures and the hottest twelve month period ever measured in the U.S., with persistent drought in vast areas of our country. *Scientific American* introduces the lead article in its special issue this month with the following sentence: 'The debate on global warming is over.'. . .

"Individual Americans of all ages are becoming a part of a movement, asking what they can do as individuals and what they can do as consumers and as citizens and voters. Many individuals and businesses have decided to take an approach known as 'Zero Carbon.'"[2]

Meanwhile, RFK had won the primaries he had contested so far: Indiana and Nebraska, beating McCarthy and Johnson/Humphrey surrogates. The next was Oregon on May 28. Then on to California.

PRESS RELEASE
Los Angeles, California, May 26, 1968

California is blessed with a bounty of land, water, climate, and scenic beauty. Millions have come here because of those natural advantages, making this state rich in industry, agriculture, and modern culture.

But in California as in the rest of America, our natural environment today is far different from what it once was. By treating our physical surroundings as an endless receptacle for human waste, we have begun to poison the air we breathe, the food we eat, the water we drink and would like to swim in. We have managed, in less than a century, to disturb the balance of nature as it had previously existed for some 40,000 years.

Of the pesticides spread across crops in California, it is estimated that about 5 percent reaches the pests; the other 95 percent goes into the air and land and water, the crops themselves, and the human beings who subsequently consume them.

Doctors performing autopsies in California have found higher levels of pesticides in human bodies than the United States government permits in beef for consumption.

In Los Angeles County, the health threat caused by air pollution due to automobile fumes is such that doctors advise more than 10,000 persons each year to move out of the area.

Hospitalization costs in Los Angeles for persons whose respiratory conditions are worsened by smog have reached $125 million annually; the damage wrought by air pollution on California's crops, forests, and plants is estimated at $240 million annually. The effect of smog in reducing the growth of crops in the state is estimated at another $110 million.

Pollution must be attacked by eliminating its sources rather than just ameliorating its effects. Faced with the need to overcome the problem or be overcome, California has led the nation in the control of motor vehicle emissions. But the need is clear for much more stringent control than now exists. California's efforts toward this end would receive the aid and cooperation of the federal government if I am elected President. . . .

Attempts to control the pollution of our water and atmosphere cannot be allowed to fail. The environment in which we live is part of us; when we degrade it, we degrade ourselves. . . .

▤ 24 ▤

Victory

O N MAY 28, OREGON handed RFK his first electoral defeat, with Eugene McCarthy winning 44.7 percent to Kennedy's 38.8. The Kennedy camp had known Oregon would be easier for McCarthy, since the state was largely middle-class and white. As he campaigned there, Kennedy seemed off his game, and avoided debating McCarthy. California, site of the next primary, was a different story. The crowds for Kennedy, often largely black or Mexican American, were huge and enthusiastic.

One evening, Kennedy met with black militants in Oakland. According to John Seigenthaler, a Kennedy adviser, it was a "rough, gut-cutting meeting in which a handful of people stood up and blistered white society and him as a symbol of white society." The berating went on and on. A local man known as Black Jesus said, "I don't want to hear none of your shit. What the goddamned hell are you going to do, boy? . . . You bastards haven't did nothing for us." On the way back to San Francisco, RFK said to Seigenthaler, "I'm glad I went. . . . They need to know somebody who'll listen . . . after all the abuse the blacks have taken through the centuries, whites are just going to have to let them get some of these feelings out if we are all really ever going to settle down to a decent relationship."[1]

The next morning, RFK went back to Oakland for a rally. Black Jesus had circulated a leaflet telling the crowd that Kennedy should be treated with the "utmost respect." As Schlesinger tells it, when RFK "finished, the crowd swarmed around the car, reaching out to touch him. The car could not move so, said Black Jesus, 'I walked in front of the car and raised my hand, and they parted so we could get through.'"[2]

On June 1, Los Angeles hosted the first and only debate between Kennedy and McCarthy. Humphrey had been asked but he declined. McCarthy had a reputation for eloquence and was favored to win, but he spent the hours before the debate not studying the issues but hanging out with friends, including the poet Robert Lowell, making literary jokes and composing impromptu poems. It was no wonder that during the debate McCarthy seemed at times abstracted and unprepared. Neither he nor Kennedy scored a knockout, which, given the higher expectations for McCarthy's performance, made Kennedy the winner. A *Los Angeles Times* telephone poll of voters agreed.[3]

On June 4, Kennedy won both primaries, in South Dakota, the most rural state in the nation, and California, the most urban. In California, Kennedy won 46.3 percent of the vote, McCarthy 41.8 percent, and the Humphrey slate headed by the state attorney general 11.9 percent. South Dakota, where Humphrey had been born and which is next to Minnesota, which both Humphrey and

McCarthy had served as senators, gave Kennedy more than 50 percent. He was happy about the results in a Native American precinct: 878 votes for Kennedy, 9 for the Johnson-Humphrey slate, 2 for McCarthy. He had won five out of six primaries. He was expected to win his home state of New York on June 19.[4]

Humphrey had not won any delegates through direct vote, but he was already ahead because of delegates appointed by a party organization still largely controlled by Johnson. That night, the breakdown of delegates had Humphrey with 944; Kennedy, 524; McCarthy, 204; undecided, 872.[5] RFK's next step was to convince McCarthy to drop out, probably by offering him the post of Secretary of State in a Kennedy administration.[6] Kennedy would then make the case to the country that he had gone to the people, via the primary process, and won the most delegate votes in the most democratic way, whereas Humphrey was gaining delegates through behind-the-scenes agreements with political bosses. Kennedy's goal by convention time was to have 1,432 delegates, while Humphrey would have only 1,152.

CALIFORNIA VICTORY SPEECH
AMBASSADOR HOTEL BALLROOM
Los Angeles, California, June 4, 1968

I am grateful to the people of California and to the people of South Dakota for the confidence in my candidacy which they have demonstrated through today's victories.

If there is one clear lesson of this political year it is that the people of this country wish to move away from the policies which have led us to an endless war abroad and to increasing unrest in our own country. Senator McCarthy demonstrated this in New Hampshire and Wisconsin. He and his supporters deserve the gratitude of the nation for the courageous fight which helped break the political logjam, demonstrated the desire for change, and helped make citizen participation into a new and powerful force of our political life. In the primaries up to now he and I have sought the popular judgement as to which of us should lead the forces of change. That decision has now been made. For it is clear tonight, as it has been for some time, that only the victor in the California primary could hope to win the Democratic nomination.

Vice President Humphrey now appears to be leading in the contest for the nomination. Yet I do not think he will be successful. In every primary, in Wisconsin and Indiana, Nebraska and Oregon, California and South Dakota, the people have rejected by more than four to one those slates committed to the Johnson-Humphrey Administration. More than eighty percent of the vote has gone to Senator McCarthy or myself, although we both reject those policies which the Vice President so fervently advocates.

I cannot believe that the Democratic Party will nominate a man whose ideas and programs have been so decisively rejected. Yet the Vice President apparently believes he can win the nomination without once submitting his case to the people. I do not believe the Presidential nomination can be a private affair. Yet the Vice President refused to enter his name in primaries, while helping delegates opposed to my candidacy. He has refused to participate in any direct confrontation on the issues. Certainly the Vice President cannot hope to be nominated without once discussing the important problems of his country with his opponents, without subjecting himself, if not to popular vote, to a popular judgement. For my part, I will go any place any time to meet the Vice President in a televised debate.

To those who have supported Senator McCarthy I have only this to say: You have fought well for principles in which you believed. In my judgment, I now remain the only candidate who can be nominated who is also in substantial agreement with those principles. In particular, I am the only candidate committed to a realistic negotiated solution to the Vietnamese war, one embracing all the elements of the South Vietnamese population and opposed to the use of American military force to carry the major burden of what should be essentially a Vietnamese conflict. In fact, I am the only candidate with policies likely to bring an honorable peace to let the killing stop.

Yet the forces against this position are so powerful, I do not believe I can be successful without your help and support. I ask this, not for myself, but for the cause and the ideas which moved you to begin this great popular movement. If we are divided then those who will benefit are those who wish to keep the policies of the past five years. . . . With you I know we can keep faith with the American need and the American desire for peace and for justice and for a government dedicated to giving the people mastery over their affairs and future.

I am very grateful for the votes that I received—that all of you worked for . . . in the agricultural areas of the state, as well as in the cities . . . as well as in the suburbs. I think it indicates quite clearly what we can do here in the United States. The vote here in the state of California, the vote in the state of South Dakota: Here in the most urban state of any of the states of our union, and South Dakota, the most rural state of any of the states of our union. We were able to win them both.

I think we can end the divisions within the United States. What I think is quite clear is that we can work together in the last analysis. And that what has been going on with the United States over the period of the last three years—the divisions, the violence, the disenchantment with our society, the divisions, whether it's between blacks and whites, between the poor and the more affluent, or between age groups, or over the war in Vietnam—that we can start to work together again. We are a great country, an unselfish country, and a compassionate country. And I intend to make that my basis for running over the period of the next few months. . . .

So my thanks to all of you, and it's on to Chicago, and let's win there.

There were shouts and applause.

RFK left the stage.

He walked through the hotel kitchen, shaking workers' hands.

A man he didn't know, Sirhan Sirhan, shot him.

RFK fell to the floor.

Mrs. Kennedy leaned over her husband.

He asked, "Is everybody else all right?" then lost consciousness and never regained it.[7]

He died twenty-six hours later.

Robert Francis Kennedy's coffin lay in St. Patrick's Cathedral in New York City for two days. Tens of thousands waited in a line a mile long to pay their last respects. At the requiem mass on June 8, the New York Philharmonic under Leonard Bernstein played Handel and Mahler, and Andy Williams sang "The Battle Hymn of the Republic."

Bobby's younger brother, Senator Edward Kennedy, gave the eulogy:

On behalf of Mrs. Robert Kennedy, her children and the parents and sisters of Robert Kennedy, I want to express what we feel to those who mourn with us today in this Cathedral and around the world. We loved him as a brother and father and son. From his parents, and from his older brothers and sisters—Joe, Kathleen and Jack—he received inspiration which he passed on to all of us. He gave us strength in time of trouble, wisdom in time of uncertainty, and sharing in time of happiness. He was always by our side.

Love is not an easy feeling to put into words. Nor is loyalty, or trust or joy. But he was all of these. He loved life completely and lived it intensely.

A few years back, Robert Kennedy wrote some words about his own father and they expressed the way we in his family feel about him. He said of what his father meant to him: "What it really all adds up to is love—not love as it is described with such facility in popular magazines, but the kind of love that is affection and respect, order, encouragement, and support. Our awareness of this was an incalculable source of strength, and because real love is something unselfish and involves sacrifice and giving, we could not help but profit from it.

"Beneath it all, he has tried to engender a social conscience. There were wrongs which needed attention. There were people who were poor and who needed help. And we have a responsibility to them and to this country. Through no virtues and accomplishments of our own, we have been fortunate enough to be born in the United States under the most comfortable conditions. We, therefore, have a responsibility to others who are less well off."

This is what Robert Kennedy was given. What he leaves us is what he said, what he did and what he stood for. A speech he made to the young people of South Africa on their Day of Affirmation in 1966 sums it up the best, and I would read it now:

"There is a discrimination in this world and slavery and slaughter and starvation. Governments repress their people; and millions are trapped in poverty while the nation grows rich; and wealth is lavished on armaments everywhere.

"These are differing evils, but they are common works of man. They reflect the imperfection of human justice, the inadequacy of human compassion, our lack of sensibility toward the sufferings of our fellows.

"But we can perhaps remember—even if only for a time—that those who live with us are our brothers; that they share with us the same short moment of life; that they seek—as we do—nothing but the chance to live out their lives in purpose and happiness, winning what satisfaction and fulfillment they can.

"Surely this bond of common faith, this bond of common goal, can begin to teach us something. Surely, we can learn, at least, to look at those around us as fellow men. And surely we can begin to work a little harder to bind up the wounds among us and to become in our own hearts brothers and countrymen once again.

"Our answer is to rely on youth—not a time of life but a state of mind, a temper of the will, a quality of imagination, a predominance of courage over timidity, of the appetite for adventure over the love of ease. The cruelties and obstacles of this swiftly changing planet will not yield to obsolete dogmas and outworn slogans. They cannot be moved by those who cling to a present that is already dying, who prefer the illusion of security to the excitement and danger that come with even the most peaceful progress. It is a revolutionary world we live in; and this generation at home and around the world, has had thrust upon it a greater burden of responsibility than any generation that has ever lived.

"Some believe there is nothing one man or one woman can do against the enormous array of the world's ills. Yet many of the world's great movements, of thought and action, have flowed from the work of a single man. A young monk began the Protestant reformation, a young general extended an empire from Macedonia to the borders of the earth, and a young woman reclaimed the territory of France. It was a young Italian explorer who discovered the New World, and the thirty-two-year-old Thomas Jefferson who proclaimed that all men are created equal.

"These men moved the world, and so can we all. Few will have the greatness to bend history itself, but each of us can work to change a small portion of events, and in the total of all those acts will be written the history of this generation. It is from numberless diverse acts of courage and belief that human history is shaped. Each time a man stands up for an ideal, or acts to improve the lot of others, or strikes out against injustice, he sends forth a tiny ripple of hope, and crossing each other from a million different centers of energy and daring, those ripples build a current that can sweep down the mightiest walls of oppression and resistance.

"Few are willing to brave the disapproval of their fellows, the censure of their colleagues, the wrath of their society. Moral courage is a rarer commodity than bravery in battle or great intelligence. Yet it is the one essential, vital quality for those who seek to change a world that yields most painfully to change. And I believe that in this generation those with the courage to enter the moral conflict will find themselves with companions in every corner of the globe.

"For the fortunate among us, there is the temptation to follow the easy and familiar paths of personal ambition and financial success so grandly spread before those who enjoy the privilege of education. But that is not the road history has marked out for us. Like it or not, we live in times of danger and uncertainty. But they are also more open to the creative energy of men than any other time in history. All of us will ultimately be judged and as the years pass we will surely judge ourselves, on the effort we have contributed to building a new world society and the extent to which our ideals and goals have shaped that effort.

"The future does not belong to those who are content with today, apathetic toward common problems and their fellow man alike, timid and fearful in the face of new ideas and bold projects. Rather it will belong to those who can blend vision, reason and courage in a personal commitment to the ideals and great enterprises of American Society.

"Our future may lie beyond our vision, but it is not completely beyond our control. It is the shaping impulse of America that neither fate nor nature nor the irresistible tides of history, but the work of our own hands, matched to reason and principle, that will determine our destiny. There is pride in that, even arrogance, but there is also experience and truth. In any event, it is the only way we can live."

This is the way he lived. My brother need not be idealized, or enlarged in death beyond what he was in life, to be remembered simply as a good and decent man, who saw wrong and tried to right it, saw suffering and tried to heal it, saw war and tried to stop it.

Those of us who loved him and who take him to his rest today, pray that what he was to us and what he wished for others will some day come to pass for all the world.

As he said many times, in many parts of this nation, to those he touched and who sought to touch him:

"Some men see things as they are and ask why. I dream things that never were and ask why not."[8]

A million people lined the tracks as a Pennsylvania Railroad train carried RFK's body from New York to Washington.

At his grave in Arlington National Cemetery, lines from two of his speeches are etched in marble. There is the Aeschylus:

"In our sleep, pain which cannot forget falls drop by drop upon the heart until, in our own despair, against our will, comes wisdom through the awful grace of God."

The other passage is from the address he gave in 1966 in South Africa to honor the struggle for freedom of the black population there, and which his brother quoted in the eulogy:

"It is from numberless diverse acts of courage and belief that human history is shaped. Each time a man stands up for an ideal, or acts to improve the lot of others, or strikes out against injustice, he sends forth a tiny ripple of hope, and crossing each other from a million different centers of energy and daring, those ripples build a current which can sweep down the mightiest walls of oppression and resistance."

ACKNOWLEDGMENTS

I have been thinking about this project since 1993—originally as a documentary film, using just the footage of the speeches made by RFK in his 1968 campaign. I would still like to make such a film, for so much is conveyed in the crowds, and the delivery: Kennedy on film is tough, childlike, sad, frail, indomitable, and often very funny.

From the film flowed the idea of a documentary book—just the speeches: they would speak for themselves. But my editor, Jill Rothenberg, convinced me that context should be provided, and not only the context of 1968. Her first major suggestion to me was the subtitle "Why It Matters Now." I cannot begin to thank her for her initial wisdom and subsequent, inspired editorial guidance. And I want to thank Holly Hodder, Westview Press, Marco Pavio, and the Perseus Books Group for their belief in this book.

For this new edition, I thank John Sherer, Courtney Miller, Robert Kimzey, Lara Heimert, and Chris Greenberg of Basic Books.

I am grateful to the John Fitzgerald Kennedy Library's staff, especially Stephen Plotkin, James B. Hill, and Michael Desmond, for their help.

Thanks to Professor James Crown of New York University for research suggestions.

Thanks to Regina Crimmins for friendship and news of the world.

Thanks to Sam and Nina Adams, Lee Fahnestock, Rebecca Campbell, Regina Haines, Marshall Efron and Alfa-Betty Olsen, Mermie Karger, Carole Chase, Donald Gordon, Sarah Blumenfeld, Stephen Paul Miller, Denise Duhamel, Mark Woods, Michael Annis, William Allen, and Robert Shogan.

I thank, as always, my partner, Dr. Miguel Cervantes-Cervantes.

I also thank Jeffrey Buchanan, communications officer at the Robert F. Kennedy Memorial in Washington, D.C., Kerry Kennedy, director. The Memorial is dedicated to advancing human rights around the world. http://www.rfkmemorial.org/.

NOTES

Speeches are courtesy of the Robert F. Kennedy Senate Files Archive in the John Fitzgerald Kennedy Library, in Boston, Massachusetts, part of the National Archives; and the Robert F. Kennedy Memorial, in Washington, D.C.

INTRODUCTION

1. Jack Newfield, *RFK: A Memoir* (New York: Thunder's Mouth Press/Nation Books, 1969, 1978, 1988, 2003), p. 10.

2. Evan Thomas, *Robert Kennedy: His Life* (New York: Simon and Schuster, 2000), p. 376.

3. Jim Webb, "Class Struggle," *Wall Street Journal*, November 15, 2006.

4. Thomas, pp. 22, 319.

5. David Talbot, "Warrior for Peace," *Time*, June 21, 2007. See also Talbot, *Brothers: The Hidden History of the Kennedy Years* (New York: Free Press, 2007).

6. Thomas, p. 280.

7. Arthur Schlesinger, Jr., *Robert Kennedy and His Times* (New York: Ballantine, 1978), p. 941

8. Ibid., p. 862.

9. Newfield, p. 46.

10. Schlesinger, p. 852; and Arthur M. Schlesinger, Jr., *Journals, 1952–2000* (New York: Penguin Press, 2007), p. 291.

11. Thomas Jefferson, *The Jefferson Bible: The Life and Morals of Jesus,* introduction by Forrest Church (Boston: Beacon Press, 1989). Available also on the internet: www.angelfire.com/co/JeffersonBible/JeffBible.txt.

12. Pier Paolo Pasolini, *The Gospel According to Saint Matthew,* video and DVD (Rome: 1964; New York: Museum of Modern Art/Waterbearer Films, 2003).

13. *RFK: Collected Speeches,* edited by Edwin O. Guthman and C. Richard Allen (New York: Viking, 1993).

14. In Norman MacAfee, *One Class* (Brownsville, Vt.: Harbor Mountain Press, 2008).

CHAPTER 1

1. Edward Sanders, *1968: A History in Verse* (Santa Rosa, Calif.: Black Sparrow Press, 1997), p. 49.

2. Robert F. Kennedy, *Thirteen Days: A Memoir of the Cuban Missile Crisis* (New York: Norton, 1969, 1971; with new foreword by Arthur Schlesinger, Jr., 1999), especially pp. 76–79.

3. Barbara Garson, *MacBird!* (New York: Grove Press, 1967).

4. Mark Kurlansky, *1968: The Year That Rocked the World* (New York: Ballantine, 2004), p. 107.

CHAPTER 2

1. Kurlansky, *1968,* pp. 60–61.

2. Newfield, p. 234.

3. "Senator Edward Kennedy Says U.S. Case for War Against Iraq Was a 'Fraud,'" interview with Kennedy in Associated Press, September 18, 2003.

CHAPTER 3

1. Peter Edelman, *Searching for America's Heart: RFK and the Renewal of Hope* (Washington, D.C.: Georgetown University Press, 2003), pp. 52–53.

2. Thomas, p. 280.

3. Newfield, p. 8.

4. Paul Krugman, *The Great Unraveling* (New York: Norton, 2003), pp. 220–221.

5. Webb, "Class Struggle."

CHAPTER 4

1. Al Gore, Vanderbilt University, February 8, 2004.

CHAPTER 6

1. Schlesinger, p. 929.

2. Newfield, pp. 241–242.

CHAPTER 7

1. Schlesinger, *Robert Kennedy and His Times*, p. 824.

CHAPTER 8

1. Schlesinger, *Robert Kennedy and His Times*, pp. 853–854.

2. Ibid., p. 852. The Kennedy quote is from Robert F. Kennedy, "Crisis in Our Cities," *The Critic*, November/December 1967.

3. Ibid.

CHAPTER 9

1. *RFK: Collected Speeches*, pp. 341–342.

2. Thomas, p. 370.

3. Schlesinger, *Robert Kennedy and His Times*, p. 901, quoting Jeffrey Potter, *Men, Money, and Magic* (New York: Coward, McCann, and Geoheghan, 1976), pp. 308–309.

CHAPTER 10

1. Newfield, p. 243.

2. Doris Kearns Goodwin, *Lyndon Johnson and the American Dream* (New York: St. Martin's, 1976), p. 343, via Schlesinger, *Robert Kennedy and His Times*, p. 931.

3. Newfield, p. 243.

CHAPTER 11

1. Edelman, p. 7.
2. Schlesinger, *Robert Kennedy and His Times*, p. 863.
3. Thomas, p. 319.
4. Thomas, pp. 325–326.

CHAPTER 12

1. Sanders, *1968: A History in Verse*, p. 77.
2. Thomas, p. 368.

CHAPTER 13

1. Schlesinger, *Robert Kennedy and His Times*, p. 941.

CHAPTER 14

1. Schlesinger, *Robert Kennedy and His Times*, p. 944.
2. Ibid., p. 943.

CHAPTER 15

1. Kennedy, *Thirteen Days*, pp. 76–79.
2. Ibid., p. 11.

CHAPTER 16

1. www.restorationplaza.org.
2. Thomas, p. 342; Edelman, p. 104.
3. Edelman, p. 104.
4. www.restorationplaza.org.

CHAPTER 17

1. Trudy Lieberman, "Hungry in America," *The Nation,* July 31, 2003, www.thenation.com.

CHAPTER 19

1. Senator Edward M. Kennedy Introduces the Health Security and Affordability Act, January 22, 2004, Statement of Senator Edward M. Kennedy, An American Health Care Agenda Families USA Annual Health Care Conference.

2. Jules Witcover, *85 Days: The Last Campaign of Robert Kennedy* (New York: Putnam, 1969), p. 165, quoted by Schlesinger, *Robert Kennedy and His Times,* p. 948.

CHAPTER 20

1. Thomas, p. 376.

2. Schlesinger, *Robert Kennedy and His Times,* pp. 956–957.

3. Ibid., p. 957, quoting Richard Harwood, remarks at RFK Journalism Awards' luncheon, Washington, D.C., May 14, 1976.

4. Schlesinger, *Robert Kennedy and His Times,* p. 971.

CHAPTER 21

1. Newfield, p. 59.

2. Edelman, p. 10.

CHAPTER 22

1. Thomas, pp. 363–364.

2. Edelman, pp. 6–7.

CHAPTER 23

1. Robert F. Kennedy, Jr., "Crimes Against Nature," *Rolling Stone,* December 11, 2003.

2. Al Gore, speech at New York University Law School, September 18, 2006.

CHAPTER 24

1. Jean Stein and George Plimpton, eds., *American Journey* (New York: Harcourt, 1970), p. 305.

2. Schlesinger, *Robert Kennedy and His Times*, pp. 975–976.

3. Ibid., pp. 978–979.

4. Thomas, p. 388.

5. Schlesinger, *Robert Kennedy and His Times,* p. 981.

6. Thomas, p. 388.

7. Ibid., p. 391.

8. Robert F. Kennedy Memorial, http://www.rfkmemorial.org/lifevision/tributetosenatorrfk/.

BIBLIOGRAPHY

The texts of the speeches of Robert Kennedy were made from copies in the collection at the John Fitzgerald Kennedy Library. I would like to acknowledge Edwin O. Guthman and C. Richard Allen's invaluable book, *RFK: Collected Speeches,* where I first encountered many of the speeches in this volume. As the title indicates, *RFK: Collected Speeches* includes speeches from Kennedy's entire public career, from a 1955 lecture at Georgetown through the Senate Rackets Committee Hearings of 1956–1959, the presidential campaign of his brother in 1960, through his time as attorney general, senator, and presidential candidate. The speechwriters included Adam Walinsky, Peter Edelman, Richard Goodwin, Theodore Sorenson, and Jeff Greenfield.

BOOKS

Peter Edelman, *Searching for America's Heart: RFK and the Renewal of Hope* (Washington, D.C.: Georgetown University Press, 2003).

Bill Eppridge, photographer, *Robert Kennedy: The Last Campaign,* text by Hays Gorey, Foreword by President Bill Clinton (New York: Harcourt Brace, 1993).

Barbara Garson, *MacBird!* (New York: Grove Press, 1966, 1967).

Edwin O. Guthman and C. Richard Allen, eds., *RFK: Collected Speeches* (New York: Viking, 1993).

Thomas Jefferson, *The Jefferson Bible: The Life and Morals of Jesus,* introduction by Forrest Church (Boston: Beacon Press, 1989). Available also on the internet: www.angelfire.com/co/JeffersonBible/JeffBible.txt

Maxwell Taylor Kennedy, ed., *Make Gentle the Life of This World: The Vision of Robert F. Kennedy* (New York: Harcourt Brace, 1998).

Robert F. Kennedy, *Thirteen Days: A Memoir of the Cuban Missile Crisis* (New York: Norton, 1969, 1971; with new foreword by Arthur Schlesinger, Jr., 1999).

———, *To Seek a Newer World* (New York: Bantam, 1967).

Paul Krugman, *The Great Unraveling: Losing Our Way in the New Century* (New York: Norton, 2003).

Mark Kurlansky, *1968: The Year That Rocked the World* (New York: Ballantine, 2004).

Jack Newfield, *RFK: A Memoir* (New York: Thunder's Mouth Press/ Nation Books, 1969, 1978, 1988, 2003).

Edward Sanders, *1968: A History in Verse* (Santa Rosa, Calif: Black Sparrow Press, 1997).

Arthur Schlesinger, Jr., *Journals, 1952–2000* (New York: Penguin Press, 2007).

———, *Robert Kennedy and His Times* (New York: Ballantine, 1978).

———, *A Thousand Days: John F. Kennedy in the White House* (Boston: Houghton Mifflin, 1965, 1993, 2002).

David Talbot, *Brothers: The Hidden History of the Kennedy Years* (New York: Free Press, 2007).

Evan Thomas, *Robert Kennedy: His Life* (New York: Simon and Schuster, 2000).

Videos

The Speeches of Robert F. Kennedy, The Speeches Collection, MPI Home
Video, 1990.

Pier Paolo Pasolini, *The Gospel According to Saint Matthew,* VHS and DVD
(Rome: 1964; New York: Museum of Modern Art/Waterbearer Films,
2003).

Index

Abernathy, Ralph, 107
Adams, John, 154
Aeschylus, 5, 98, 180
African-Americans, 3, 53, 79, 80, 97, 107–115, 140, 144, 166, 169, 174
Agriculture, 145–150, 166
Air pollution, 44, 143, 149, 150, 163–167
Alabama, University of, RFK at, 53–57
Allen, C. Richard, 8–9
Ambassador Hotel, 171–175
Antiwar movement, 2, 14, 15, 41–42, 49, 80
Appalachia, 44, 50, 56
Aristotle, 141
Arlington National Cemetery, 180
Arms race, 122
Australia, 69

Bedford-Stuyvesant, 61, 90–94, 125–128
Bedford-Stuyvesant Development and Services Corporation, 91, 92
Bedford-Stuyvesant Restoration Corporation, 90, 91, 92, 93, 125–128
Belafonte, Harry, 9
Bernstein, Leonard, 175
Bevel, James, 107
Bill of Rights, 82
Black, Hugo, 54
Black Jesus, 169, 170
Blake, William, 11
Branigan, Roger, 145
Breslin, Jimmy, 158
Brookings, South Dakota, 149–150
Brooklyn, NY, 90, 125–128
Bundy, McGeorge, 90

Bush, George H. W., 23
Bush, George W., 23–24, 48, 163

California primary, 170, 171, 174
Cambodia, 7, 134
Camus, Albert, 4, 14, 51, 151
Carter, Jimmy, 107
CBS News, 21
Chávez, César, 6, 73–77
Cheney, Dick, 24
Chile, 5, 7
China, 123
Citizens' Board of Inquiry into Health and Nutrition in the United States, report of, 129–132
City Club of Cleveland, RFK at, 102–105
Civil rights, 2, 13, 23, 48, 95
Class, 3, 11, 40, 54, 79
Clinton, Bill, 139, 152, 158
Clinton, Hillary, 9, 139
Cold War, 139
Colonialism, 134
Columbia University, student strike at, 2
Committee for the Preservation of the Nation, 30
Communism, 117–118, 122, 134

Community corporations, 90, 91, 125–128
Community development, 89–94, 160
Community projects, 127, 143
Compassion, 45, 66, 67, 113, 174, 176
Conservatism, 161, 162
Constitution, U.S., 82
Cooperation, 48, 62, 91
Corruption, 25, 28, 29–30, 65
Courage, 45, 180
Credibility gap, 85
"Crisis in Our Cities" (RFK), 74
Cronkite, Walter, 21–22
Cuban missile crisis, 13, 17, 63, 117, 118–119
Custer Died for Your Sins (Deloria), 73

Daley, Richard, 158
Dante, 14
de Gaulle, Charles, 69
Dean, Howard, 60
Debate, importance of, 49, 50
Declaration of Independence, 82, 117
Deloria, Vine, Jr., 73
Democratic National Committee, 60

Democratic National Convention, 18

Democratic Party, 53, 60, 64, 80–81, 83, 145

Department of Labor, 112

Dien Bien Phu, 69

Dignity, 56, 57, 64, 75, 108, 113, 114, 137, 160

Dillon, Douglas, 91

Discrimination, 48, 110, 176

Dissent, 3, 47, 49, 50, 51

Diversity, 121–122, 149

Doar, John, 91

Drinan, Father Robert, 9

Drugs, 42, 63

Dubcek, Alexander, 1

Earth Day, 163

Economic conditions, 54, 112, 127, 149

Edelman, Peter, 89, 151–152, 158

Education, 6, 18, 45, 60, 65, 76, 81, 83, 110, 111, 113, 115, 130

Einstein, Albert, 144

Ellison, Ralph, 154

Emerson, Ralph Waldo, 4, 161

Environmental issues, 44–45, 65, 163–167

Equality, 5, 8, 44, 76, 112, 178

Food stamps, 39, 131

"For Robert Kennedy's 80th Birthday Celebration" (MacAfee), 9–11

Ford, Gerald, 7

Ford Foundation, 90

France, 69, 82, 118

Freedom, 8, 54, 81, 123, 150, 159, 161, 180

Freeman, Orville, 39

Gandhi, Mohandas, 74, 95

Gap between rich and poor, 3, 40

Gardiner, Arthur, 28

Gardner, John, 41

Garson, Barbara, 14–15

Ghettoes, 39, 50, 110, 111–112, 113, 114, 144

Global warming, 164, 165

Goodwin, Doris Kearns, 85

Gore, Al, 47–48, 158, 164

Gospel According to Saint Matthew, The (film), 8

Great Depression, 111

Great Society, 2, 23

Greenfield, Jeff, 9

Greenhouse gases, 164

Guinea, 119–120

Guthman, Edwin O., 8–9

Handel, George Frideric, 175
Halliburton, 24
Harris, Fred, 73
Harwood, Richard, 146
Health care, 6, 18, 45, 65, 139–144, 161, 166
Health Security and Affordability Act, 139–140
Ho Chi Minh, 1, 23, 82
Housing, 61, 111, 126, 147, 160
Hudson River, reclamation of, 164
Huerta, Dolores, 9
Humphrey, Hubert Horatio, 6, 26–27, 53, 107, 145, 165, 170, 171, 172
Hunger, 39, 51, 129–132, 143, 148
Hussein, Saddam, 23, 24, 48

IBM, 125–128
Idaho State University, 79
Indiana primary, 145
Indiana University, 133–137
Indiana University Medical School, 140–144
Indianapolis, 96, 97–99
Infant mortality, 130, 147
Injustice, 143, 178, 180
Institute for Strategic Studies, 120
Integration, racial, 53

International Voluntary Services, 28
Iraq, invasion of, 23–24, 48

Jefferson, Thomas, 8, 37, 45, 50, 62, 81, 83, 178
Jesus, 7, 8
Jobs, 112, 113, 114, 123, 143, 148, 149–150, 155, 160
John Fitzgerald Kennedy Library, 8
Johnson, Lyndon Baines, 2, 4, 13, 15, 18, 23, 24, 30, 47, 59, 60, 69, 85–88, 145, 165
Justice, 4, 5, 8, 44, 51, 56, 66, 97, 98, 104, 107, 108, 110, 120, 121, 123, 125, 135, 173, 176

Kansas, University of, RFK at, 41–45
Kansas State University, RFK speech at, 22–37
Kennedy, Edward, 9, 18, 139–140, 175–179
Kennedy, Ethel, 9, 22, 23, 175
Kennedy, Joseph, Jr., 175
Kennedy, John Fitzgerald (JFK), 3–4, 5, 6, 13, 14, 21, 36, 73, 101, 145, 175
Kennedy, Kathleen, 175
Kennedy, Kerry, 9

Kennedy, Robert Francis (RFK)
   campaign of, 2–3, 7, 9, 16, 22,
      40, 47, 59
   death of, 1, 6, 7, 8, 11, 175
   JFK and, 6, 13, 73, 101
   LBJ and, 13, 15, 18, 47, 60, 85
Kennedy, Robert F., Jr., 163,
   164
Kerry, John, 9
Khe Sanh, 29
Khrushchev, Nikita, 118
King, Coretta Scott, 5, 101
King, Martin Luther, Jr., 4–5,
   95–99, 101, 107, 108, 145
Krugman, Paul, 40
Kucinich, Dennis, 9

Land reform, 28, 29
Leadership, 44, 61, 62, 63, 66, 90,
   158, 162
Lee, Spike, 126
Lerner, Rabbi Michael, 9
Lewis, John, 9
Liberalism, 89, 161, 162
Liddell Hart, Basil, 119
Lincoln, Abraham, 103, 155
Longworth, Alice Roosevelt, 5
Los Angeles Times, 170
Lota coal mines, Chile, 5–6
Lowell, Robert, 170

Macbeth (Shakespeare), 14
MacBird! (Garson), 14–15
Mahler, Gustav, 175
Malnutrition, 129–132
Malraux, André, 69
Mao Zedong, 82
Markey, Edward, 9
Marx, Karl, 82
McCarthy, Eugene, 15, 17, 18, 59,
      80, 107, 146, 147, 165, 169,
      170, 171, 172
McCarthy, Joseph, 89, 145
Medicaid, 141
Medicare, 89, 140, 141, 160
Mexican-Americans, 56, 74, 75,
      76, 79, 111, 169
Michigan State University,
   110–115
Military draft, 59, 79
Mississippi Delta, 39, 43, 50
Mitterrand, François, 69
Monterey, California, 70–71
Moore, George, 91
Morality and ethics, 8, 33, 35, 37,
      121, 141, 178
My Lai massacre, 13, 15–16

National Farm Workers
   Association, 73
National Guard, 101

National Liberation Front, 35–36, 83

National reconciliation, 53–57, 60

National Security Council, 17

Nationalism, 122, 133, 136

Native Americans, 3, 17, 39, 43, 50, 56, 73, 171

Nebraska primary, 146

Neoconservatives, 60

New Democrats, 158

New politics, RFK and, 157–162

New York Philharmonic, 175

Newfield, Jack, 5, 50, 59, 86

9/11, 24, 48

Nixon, Richard, 6, 7, 53, 80, 83, 107

Norris, George, 54

Nuclear Test Ban Treaty, 17, 117

Nuclear weapons, 118, 119, 164

Obama, Barack, 9

Oklahomans for Indian Opportunity, 73

Oregon primary, 169

Otoe County Courthouse, Nebraska, RFK at, 147–148

Overseas Press Club, RFK at, 86–88

Pacification program, 26–27, 29

Pasolini, Pier Paolo, 8

Patriotism, 81, 155

Peace, 4, 25, 33, 34, 63, 66, 86, 87–88, 97, 109, 110, 115, 117–123, 125, 173, 177

Peace Corps, 42, 49, 63

Pelosi, Nancy, 9

Pesticides, 166

Pol Pot, 7

Pollution, 44, 143, 149, 150, 163–167

Poverty, 1, 3, 4, 11, 16, 39–40, 44, 50, 62, 89, 110, 115, 143, 144, 148, 152, 155, 174, 176

President's Commission on Civil Disorders, 42

Press Gang, 158–162

Public assistance, 152–153, 160

Pueblo (U.S.S.), 33

Race, 3, 48, 53–54, 62, 107, 108, 110, 113

Reagan, Ronald, 23

Refugees, 31, 32

Religion, 5, 8

Report of the Citizens' Board of Inquiry into Health and Nutrition in the United States, 129–132

Restoration Plaza, Brooklyn, 126

RFK. See Kennedy, Robert Francis

RFK: Collected Speeches (Guthman and Allen), 8–9
Riverside Church, 95
Robert Kennedy and His Times (Schlesinger), 5
Rockefeller, Nelson, 107
Rojas, Raul, 75
Roosevelt, Eleanor, 89
Roosevelt, Franklin D., 53, 54, 64, 89, 161
Roosevelt, Franklin D., Jr., 89
Roosevelt, Theodore, 5
Rural America, 145–150
Russell, Bertrand, 80

Saint Francis, 74
St. Patrick's Cathedral, RFK at, 175
St. Patrick's Day parades, 22
Salinas, California, RFK in, 70–71
Sanders, Edward, 13
Sartre, Jean-Paul, 80
Scarborough, Joe, 9
Schlesinger, Arthur, Jr., 5, 6, 73, 74, 118–119, 144, 146, 170
Scientific American, on global warming, 165
Scottish Rite Banquet Hall, RFK at, 108–110
Seeger, Pete, 164
Seigenthaler, John, 169

Selective Service, 49
Senate Committee on Government Operations, 30
Shaw, George Bernard, 125
Sihanouk, Prince, 134
Sirhan, Sirhan, 174
Social Security, 89, 140
Solis, Hilda, 9
South Dakota primary, 170, 171, 174
South Vietnamese Army, 27, 31–32
Soviet Union, 13, 119, 122
Spock, Benjamin, 80

Tacitus, 25
Talbot, David, 4
Taxes, 24, 60, 148, 153, 154, 161
Tennessee Valley Authority, 54
Tennyson, Alfred Lord, 123
Test Ban Treaty, 63
Tet offensive, 15, 32
Thirteen Days: A Memoir of the Cuban Missile Crisis (Kennedy), 118–119
Thomas, Evan, 4, 39, 90, 126, 146, 157, 158
Thomas, Frank, 91
Touré, Sékou, 119
Truman, Harry S., 64, 139

Unemployment, 43, 89, 111, 115, 143, 147, 153, 154, 160

Unilateralism, 117, 121

United Farm Workers of America, 73–74

United Kingdom, 69, 117

United Nations, 117, 122

United States AID mission, 28, 30

USA Patriot Act, 48

Vanderbilt University, RFK at, 47–51

Viet Cong, 15, 23, 27, 28, 32, 118

Vietnam war, 2, 3, 6, 7, 14, 15–16, 17, 21–24, 25, 40–42, 45, 63, 65, 75, 76, 79, 80, 82–83, 114, 117–118, 121, 133–134

Violence, 45, 97, 98, 102, 103, 109, 111, 113, 135, 174

Walinsky, Adam, 157, 158

Wallace, George, 6, 53

War on Poverty, 2, 23, 24, 89

War on Terror, so-called, 48

Watergate, 6

Watts, Mel, 9

Watts riots, 17, 146

Webb, James, 40

Weber State College, Utah, RFK at, 81–84

Welfare, 50, 56, 60, 61, 111, 115, 122, 125, 151–155, 160

Williams, Andy, 175

Williams, Hosea, 107

Wilson, Woodrow, 64

World War II, 69, 117

Young, Andrew, 107, 108

Zero Carbon, 165